THE MEN WHO DROWNED DOLGARROG

The Men Who Drowned Dolgarrog

John Lawson-Reay

First published in 2018

ISBN: 978-1-84524-286-2

Cover design: Eleri Owen

Published by Gwasg Carreg Gwalch,
12 Iard yr Orsaf, Llanrwst, Wales LL26 0EH
tel: 01492 642031
email: books@carreg-gwalch.cymru
website: www.carreg-gwalch.cymru

Dedicated to the good and kind folk of Dolgarrog, past and present, who bore adversity with typical wry Welsh humour. I feel privileged to have been able to tell their story.

Contents

Contents

Introduction

I am very much aware that I am standing on the shoulders of those historians who have gone before. In the the case of Dolgarrog I became fascinated with the story when, as a child, I saw the massive boulder field which had engulfed the village in 1925. It was only when Eric Jones and David Gwyn published their excellent book *Dolgarrog an Industrial History* in 1989 that I was able to learn about it in depth. Their book was a prime example of an academic treatise which could not be faulted on the scale and depth of the research. However it relied upon a plethora of footnotes – very handy for me in my researches but a heavy read!

Childhood Memories

I well remember, as a child in the 1940's, on a Sunday afternoon trip out in the car with my grandparents, going through Dolgarrog and seeing the massive boulders that covered the original village and being told about the dam bursting and killing a lot of people. This was less than twenty years after the event. The boulders bordering the main road were still clean and white. Since then nature has softened them with trees and mosses so that you might not even be aware of them. It is ironic that the Welsh name Dolgarrog means the 'field of the stones' and here is a an actual field of stones!

With the factory and power station on the left, higher up and on the right were the new modern houses. I was told that they had been paid for by the Daily Mail after the disaster. The story about the disaster was true, but the truth about the houses is that they were built before the deluge and the donation of £1,000 by the Daily Mail to start a fund was rejected by Harry Jack, the General Manager of the Aluminium Corporation Ltd., on the grounds that the company alone would compensate everyone for their losses. In the event, that generous donation, along with a few smaller ones was distributed informally by the local vicar and the Chief Constable to those in most need.

During WW2 my grandparents used to drive up from Llandudno, to a farm above Eglwysbach where they could buy black market eggs, bacon, chickens and freshly churned butter. I remember having a go at cranking the churn. The bacon hung from the rafters in the kitchen and a chicken would be killed to order. The reason I mention this is because there was a girl there, I could not say what her age was – but she was probably a young woman and we were told she was an orphan from the disaster. So I have actually met a survivor. Now of course they are all gone, but there are families in north Wales who still hand down stories of the events of that night.

The men who drowned Dolgarrog

It was a dark and stormy night on 2 November 1925. At 8.45 pm the Eigiau Dam burst with an almighty, earth shattering roar, torrenting millions of gallons of water and thousands of tons of giant, ice age boulders 1,000 ft down the narrow gorge onto the unsuspecting villagers of Dolgarrog, in the Conwy Valley below. By daybreak the death toll was ten adults and six children drowned by the flood waters. That is the story that has been passed down to us.

The story has been retold many times since and is almost a legend in these parts. There have been newspaper articles and photographs published at every ten year anniversary of the event. None have added anything to our knowledge of the real causes of the disaster, and I believe that the evidence points to a cover up which has persisted to this day.

How times have changed. Reports of earth quakes with thousands dead, floods and tsunamis would then have taken up a paragraph or two on the back pages of our national newspapers. Now we expect and are often able to see film and pictures of such events almost as they are happening. This story of the Dolgarrog dam disaster whilst quite insignificant by to-day's standards was front page news in all the national, local and even French newspapers. Newsreel film of it was in the local cinemas within two days! But as we shall see you can't always believe what the papers tell you, then as now!

When I started to write this book I had read all the contemporary reports and it appeared straightforward. The dam at Eigau burst leading to the collapse of the Coedty Dam which engulfed the hamlet of Porth Llwyd. After investigation of several other sources and contemporary surveys of the scene, it has turned out not to be as clear cut as they would have had us believe. The cause, the timing and the sequence of events were cleverly hidden from the public by *Y Pobl Fawr* (the Big People)!

This is a tale of professional incompetence, criminal neglect and corporate cover up. My investigations clearly show that there were several corporate villains, but the chief suspects are Ralph Freeman, the Civil Engineer who designed the dams and Henry Joseph Jack, General Manager and Company Secretary of the Aluminium Corporation

Ralph Freeman, architect of the dams

Harry Jack,
the Managing Director

Ltd which owned and was responsible for the maintenance of the dams. Known locally as Harry Jack, he was very largely a one-man show and by 1918 he had become the Managing Director of the Corporation.

The history of the Aluminium Corporation Limited was the history of Dolgarrog. The centenary of the disaster is coming up in 2025, so I decided it was time to reveal the true story, deliberately hidden, which is much more interesting than the one which has been repeated ad nauseum over the years.

Dear reader, I hope you will be informed and absorbed by the tale that I tell.

John Lawson-Reay
2018

Chapter 1

Natural Resources in the Conwy Valley

Hydro Power

The Falls at Trefriw

The whole scheme for generating hydro power at Dolgarrog was seriously flawed even before it started. It seems that the early promoters of the project saw all the picturesque torrents of water cascading down from the Carneddau mountains as being an ideal source for the generating of cheap electricity. In reality this part of north Wales does not have a reliable history of rainfall. This could be because the eastern slopes of the Carneddau range of mountains are, in effect, in the rain shadow of the massif, including Snowdon itself to the west, from whence the prevailing weather comes. Unfortunately summer droughts are not uncommon.

Tourism

The story starts in the early nineteenth century. An 1812 guide book, *The Beauties of England and Wales, Caernarvonshire* by Evans describes the Conwy Valley:

The Vale of Conwy teems with interesting prospects. It

Victorian visitors to the wonders of the Conwy Valley

> is watered by a river, whose natural beauties, as well as historic scenes, have occasioned its celebrity to be reiterated full oft in song; and adorned by all the diversity that can arise from a well wooded, highly cultivated country, contrasted with the variation of mountain scenery.

The geography of the western side of the valley is unusual in that it features a number of hanging valleys, created by the movement of ice sheets at the end of the last Ice Age. The ice in the valley at that time was over 1,000 ft deep. The results of the ice melting were steep gorges, falling 1,000 ft down from the upland lakes and tarns, creating spectacular raging torrents, cataracts and waterfalls. In fact the area was at that time described as the Rhineland of north Wales. A guide book of that era contained prints showing views which could have been in the Alps or the Rockies.

Commerce

The river Conwy had been an important artery for commerce from the early 19 Century. Initially it was only navigable by small five ton boats but by the middle of the century, with rock blasting of the river bed at Tal-y-cafn and dredging, it was opened to sea going vessels of up to a 100 tons. At its peak, up to 450 boats visited nearby Trefriw Quay annually, trading as far as Liverpool and Dublin. They shipped out grain, hides, wool, metals, sulphur from local mines, slate, stone and timber. Imports included food, wine (for the gentry), coal and lime. In 1862, 16,530 tons was traded from Trefriw. There were, additionally, quays at Coed Gwydir, Cae Coch, Maenan Abbey, Dolgarrog and Tal-y-cafn.

By 1863 an incline had been built for the slate quarries at Cedryn and Eigiau. Bankfield House, as the office, is still there on the main road through Dolgarrog.

The water pipes from the dams now run down on this incline which became essential for the construction of the

A Conwy Valley paddle steamer

Bankfield House

Cowlyd, Eigiau, Coedty Dams and other works connected with the water supplies.

By 1847 the St George Steam Packet Company started the tourist boom with a paddle steamer taking visitors up the river from Conwy to a quay at Trefriw, just a couple of miles upstream from Dolgarrog. There tourists could visit the Chalybeate Spa, which it is believed was first used by the Romans during their occupation of Wales. By the turn of the century there was a fleet of five steamers capable of carrying a thousand passengers.

Nature has taken over so much that it is hard to picture the scene as it was then. Going up stream, on the left were the rolling hills of Denbighshire, largely unchanged, whilst on the right were massive cliffs, now thickly wooded. Where the Dolgarrog boulder field is now was a hamlet called Porth Llwyd named after the gorge and falls which lay behind it.

The Quay, Trefriw

The Plas Rhaiadr Temperance Hotel

There were only about ten dwellings then, including buildings which had formerly been used as a bakehouse, farm, smithy and watermill. The name Dolgarrog, originates from the area where the torrent, the Afon Ddu, starts at Llyn Cowlyd – the deepest natural lake in Wales, and about a mile south of Porth Llwyd on the road to Trefriw. The whole area was known as the Dolgarrog Township, probably from Medieval times. The land was owned by Lord Newborough of Glynllifon.

By the 1850's, at the height of 'Railway Mania', a plan was mooted to build a branch line from Conwy along the western side of the valley, through Rowen and Dolgarrog to meet up with the existing branch line at Llanrwst on the eastern side. To cater for the expected inrush of visitors a small hotel, the Plas Rhaiadr, was built in 1861. In the event the railway was never built.

Chapter 2

Hydro-power, Tourism and Commerce

The New Dams

At this time the valley was sparsely populated with just a few scattered cottages and smallholdings. Industry was confined largely to watermills, several quarries, lead mines and an iron sulphide mine. The major change came after the fall in livestock prices in the mid nineteenth century, when the big north Wales landowners who owned most of the acreage in the area, decided to sell their estates. The coastal holiday resorts were also being developed and looking for reliable domestic water supplies, and there was clearly an abundant supply of water flowing down off the Carneddau mountain range.

First off the block were the Llandudno Improvement Commissioners, (precursors of the Llandudno Urban District Council), who planned to extract water from Llyn Dulyn, one of two tarn lakes which nestle 1,875 ft high under the slopes of Carnedd Llewelyn. Work started in 1878 on the building of a small dam and aqueduct to take the water to Llandudno. This was extremely far-sighted as Llandudno has never, to this day experienced any water shortages, even in the driest of summers. Because of the difficulty of the terrain surrounding the site, the materials had to be carried first by horse and cart and then on horse drawn sledges. The work took three hard years.

Ten years later the Sanitary Authorities of Conwy, Colwyn Bay and Glan Conwy set up a Joint Water Supply Board to build a dam at Cowlyd, an existing natural Ice Age lake. It was to be an earth bank with a central core of concrete and clay puddle 176 yards long, which raised the lake level by 13 ft so impounding 70 million gallons of water. The work took seven years which included the pipes and aqueducts that carried the water as far as Old Colwyn and Llysfaen.

Hydro Electricity and Tourism

It was becoming obvious that Snowdonia was ripe for the development of high pressure turbine hydro-electric power stations. There was no shortage of engineers and entrepeneurs willing to exploit the potential for industry and transport. Plans for hydro electric power stations were being produced. The front runner was at Cwm Dyli in the Nant Gwynant Valley below Snowdon. This was to be the key to the development of the North Wales Power and Traction Company which had the power necessary to generate hydro electric power for the proposed Porthmadoc, Beddgelert and South Snowdon Electric Railway and was also empowered to sell electricity in bulk. Cwm Dyli's main customer was to be the slate quarrying industry and it came to play an important part in the story of the ACL

In 1883 experiments with electric traction technology were being carried out at the Cae Coch Mine near Trefriw and by 1891 the Llechwedd Quarry at Blaenau Festiniog had also started a pilot scheme, while shortly afterwards the Croesor Quarry near Ffestiniog, was the first in the UK to run a successful electric mine locomotive system.

By 1900 two rival tourism plans had emerged, based on the cheap hydro electric power. In addition this power could be sold to the burgeoning coastal towns. One was to turn the Carneddau mountain range into a giant winter and summer sports complex which would have a ski slope and golf course amongst its attractions. This would be served by a steep tramway in two sections connected by a chairlift, starting at Aber falls near Llanfairfechan and finishing at the summit of Carnedd Llywelyn. The other scheme was a 'Cataract Park' at Dolgarrog. Connecting with the Conway Valley Branch Line, a passenger tramway would cross the Conwy at a point where a wharf would be built for the pleasure steamers. It would then follow the route of existing inclines and the quarry tramway track as far as Eigiau then, clinging to the side of the mountain, a funicular would carry visitors up to the summit of Carnedd Llewelyn. Neither scheme came to fruition and some might say thank goodness!

The Aluminium Corporation Ltd is established

The roots of the ACL go back to 1807 when Sir Humphrey Davy (inventor of the miner's safety lamp) discovered alumina, but it wasn't until 1887 that scientists discovered an electrochemical process for making aluminium. The alumina was called Bauxite, from the city of Les Baux at the mouth of the river Rhone, the area in France where it was mined. To make aluminium vast quantities of electricity are required to power the furnaces in the electrolytic reduction process. So the key to the cost of aluminium lies in the availability of an abundant supply of cheap electric power. Hydro electricity was clearly the front runner in this respect and in fact by 1907 the British Aluminium Corporation's plant at Foyers in Scotland was producing 2,000 tons per year using hydro power. This was at a time when the global production was in the order of 12,000 tons per annum.

In 1907 a group of businessmen, to-day we would call them the Captains of Industry, got together to form the Aluminium Syndicate Ltd. At this time the price of aluminium was £120 per ton and its prospects as a light weight metal for use in motor cars and machinery seemed very bright. They became the underwriters for the new

The first factory being built

Aluminium Corporation which was formed on the 16 April 1907. The initial plan was for a reduction plant in Dyffryn Conwy at Dolgarrog, but they also decided to build a plant at Wallsend-on-Tyne. There they were offered a very cheap rate for electricity by the Tyne Electricity Supply Company based on the relatively low cost of coal and the plentiful supply of carbon for the electrodes used in the process. The factory on Tyneside could be up and running by late 1907 thus taking advantage of the then high prices of aluminium. Dolgarrog by contrast would require more time to build both the factory and a dam for the hydro electric power. A search for an additional source of Bauxite found that there were high yielding deposits in the Var region of Provence which could be exported from Nice in ships which were empty after delivering coal to the port.

Construction starts

A quarry was opened on the south side of the Porth Llwyd

Llyn Eigiau as an Ice Age lake before development

gorge to supply the large quantities of stone that were needed for the foundations of the factory which was situated on a flood plain.

Work then began on the factory to house four turbines and six furnaces in the same building. The possibility of enlarging the capacity of Llyn Cowlyd was considered, but rejected in favour of a new dam at Llyn Eigiau which was actually then a natural lake – a remnant of the last Ice Age.

One of the pylons used to bring power to Dolgarrog from the Cwm Dyli Power Station

In the meantime an arrangement was made with The North Wales Power and Traction Company to supply electricity from their Cwm Dyli Power Station, below Snowdon, and an overhead, three phase power line was constructed over the mountains to Dolgarrog. Rotary converters were installed to convert the alternating current to direct current for the reducing furnaces. This enabled the factory to start production before the new Eigiau Dam was completed.

In 1907 a contract was signed with Messrs Bott and Stennett of Westminster, to build the dam to the plans of Ralph Freeman (then aged 27), who worked for Douglas Fox and Partners, while Harpur Brothers were engaged as the consulting engineers. It was a major and difficult undertaking. All the machinery, locomotives and most of the materials had to be winched up 1,000 ft from the valley floor on an existing 2 ft gauge quarry tramway, then a standard gauge track had to be laid up to the site. To start with the workers were accommodated in bell tents until a shanty town of corrugated tin bunk-houses was constructed near Coedty to house the 400 or so workers at the site. The

The Shooting Lodge at Eigiau, residence of the Engineer in Charge

resident engineer lived in some comfort in Cooper's Shooting Lodge nearby. The Navvy Mission established a chapel for the workers, and there were five or six grocery shops which did a roaring trade in illegal beer, sent up from the Bedol Inn at Tal-y-bont (owned by ACL). This came to an end when an undercover policeman was served. The shopkeeper was taken to court and pleaded, convincingly, that the police had connived at the practice for a long time in order to keep the navvies out of the village pub. He was fined one shilling (5p) – a slap on the wrist!

Liquidation

The Wallsend factory started production in March 1908 and Dolgarrog came on stream on 18 November by which time the price of aluminium had halved from £120 to £60 a ton. A decision was taken to close down the Wallsend furnaces until the market improved. By 2 December, just two weeks later, the Corporation went into liquidation. Work on the Eigiau Dam was stopped and the contractors, Messrs Bott and Stennett also went under – or so it was claimed. The dam by this time was almost two thirds complete.

Clearly, the whole enterprise was seriously under capitalised. Witness the fact that just prior to the collapse, the directors of ACL had been in talks with The British Aluminium Company about a possible take over. Nothing came of this. Back to the drawing board! But there were people who still had faith in the industry's potential: so step forward a Scots businessman Kenneth McKenzie Clark, who was father of the man later to become Lord Clark, the famous TV art critic, who was also briefly elected to the board in 1930 but resigned a year later. McKenzie Clark was a shareholder in ACL and he was something of a dandy and habitué of the gaming tables of Monte Carlo, but his fortune

Kenneth McKenzie Clark who rescued ACL after liquidation in 1908

had come from the Paisley thread industry. A tall, stout man with a waxed reddish moustache, swaggering and boastful he was fond of booze and cigars, but he became the saviour of the Dolgarrog Works and the village. Dipping into his own pocket he rescued the ACL from oblivion and acquired an invaluable asset in the form of the new General Manager and Company Secretary, Henry Joseph Jack, who had been appointed by the liquidators.

Chapter 3

Harry Jack arrives with big plans

The New Broom

Little is known about the early years of Harry Jack. He was a Welshman, born in Swansea in 1869 and in 1892 he was working as wine merchant in Cardiff. What he did between then and 1909 when he arrived at Dolgarrog, is obscure. What we do know is that he was a remarkable man who had vision and drive. He could charm the birds off the trees when it came to potential investors, and was far sighted on the future development of local industries. He came to control not only the ACL but also The North Wales Power and Traction Company, The Welsh Highland Railway, The Ffestiniog Railway and the Snowdon Mountain Railway, as well as other enterprises too diverse to mention. He was a County Councillor and even at one point, Chairman of the Council. How he managed as probably the only non Welsh speaking member is not recorded! His philosophy was one of caring for his workforce and ensuring that they had a standard of living unheard of previously, in this area. The development of Dolgarrog owes much to him. Having said that, he was seen to be self important and dictatorial, which may have been a good thing in many respects, but ultimately, inevitably led to his downfall.

The Second Aluminium Corporation Ltd

The second ACL was formed in 1909 to take over the assets of the first, whilst dumping its liabilities. The following February the directors travelled up the railway to Llyn Eigiau to inspect the renewed work on the dam and see the

The construction of Eigiau Dam

progress. Workers were being taken on at both factories, Wallsend started up production in June followed by Dolgarrog in September. Six furnaces were started initially with fourteen more to come on line at the rate of two a week. By November twenty furnaces were operating for the first time. Harry Jack, when addressing the directors, warned that fancy prices for aluminium were now over but with care, prosperity was possible for all concerned in its manufacture in the future and in Dolgarrog.

The Eigiau Dam was largely completed by November 1911. All the plant was removed including the railway lines except the 2 ft gauge incline through Coed Dolgarrog which the ACL bought to be used for maintenance work.

One of the first, most pressing problems was the supply of Bauxite. The ore, which comes from the Var region of France in the form of a clay material which has to be refined proved to be unsatisfactory, so a new search led by Jack and Clark was started. They found another mine at Sillans in the same region of France and took out a lease on land which enabled them to store 2,000 tons of ore at St Raphael on the south coast. They chartered a steamer to ship the first 500 tons but quite soon the demand began to outstrip the supply. The ACL registered its own company in France and installed a foreman to oversee the work on site and ensure a constant supply of Bauxite.

Although Wallsend was operating well, the ACL Board soon realised that there was no advantage in operating on two sites and decided to close that factory. The reduction furnaces were dismantled and together with the carbon plant were removed to Dolgarrog. Corrugated iron buildings with a tall steel chimney were constructed to house these.

Bauxite refining was still retained on Tyneside. In 1912 a bungalow was built at Dolgarrog to house the laboratory of the chief chemist who would check the purity of the materials coming in and also the metals produced by the furnaces. It was given the name The Sillans, after the region from whence the ore came and had a very unusual, oriental appearance. It later became a hostel for female office staff and figured in the disaster.

The chemist's laboratory later renamed The Sillans and used to accommodate female staff

Transport

Transport to and from Dolgarrog was always a problem since the factory was on the opposite side of the valley from the Conwy Valley branch railway line. Roads were narrow and in poor condition on the western side of the valley. This was largely due to the motor buses taking visitors to Trefriw and steam trucks carrying materials to and from the factory. One answer was the ACL Board's proposal in 1907, to build a standard gauge rail line linking the works to the Conwy Valley branch line at the present Dolgarrog railway halt, and with an extension to Trefriw Spa. The Board then had second thoughts, withdrew the application and bought instead a five ton Foden steam wagon. However, it became clear that there was still a need for a railway connection, so the Board submitted an amended application to the Light Railway Commissioners based on their previous plan but to be powered by electricity. The proposal went to inquiry in 1908 but although it was approved the ACL had by then gone into liquidation. The directors of the new ACL were concerned that seeking approval for railways was time consuming and that there was an urgent need for a reliable method of getting raw materials into and product out of Dolgarrog.

The Anna Olga*, Russian whaling ship*

The Board decided to make use of the river Conwy by buying a fleet of secondhand vessels. The first was an old Russian Whaling ship which was to be used as a floating warehouse in Conwy Harbour, also a 40 ton steamboat named the Pioneer. These were followed by a steam barge Gorrey and a collection of unpowered barges. An agreement was reached with the London & North Western Railway to use the Ynys Quay, located close to Stephenson's Rail Tunnel Bridge at Conwy. A locomotive crane was also installed. At Dolgarrog a 2 ft gauge tramway was built between a wharf on the river bank and the works to trans-ship the materials. A stationary electric motor was used to haul the trucks but this proved to be a very laborious method, so in May 1913 work was started on building a canal from the river right up to a wharf

Barge Corporation *at the factory quay*

The works from the riverside

The canal built to connect the factory to Afon Conwy

beside the factory, this was completed by October and still exists. The canal meant that heavy loads could be moved with ease and was quite an improvement over steam lorries negotiating the narrow roads to either the Llanrwst or Tal-y-cafn goods yards. Other plans were put forward for a narrow gauge rail line from Conwy up through Henryd, Rowen and Tal-y-bont to Dolgarrog, hence to Trefriw and terminating at Llanrwst. Variations of these plans were promoted, but in 1914 the outbreak of WW1 put an end on any of these schemes.

Chapter 4

Development of the village and WW1

Development of the Village

While all this was going on, Dolgarrog the village, was developing adjacent to the factory. There was a problem with accommodating the workers locally as many had to travel from other outlying villages. So in 1911 ACL hired a

The main entrance to the factory

local building contractor, J. B. Gorst to build 20 'model cottages' at a total cost of £2,000, to accommodate the skilled furnacemen, who had been recruited from Scotland. The first ten of these were built along the main road opposite the factory (known as Croft Cottages) and a further ten on Hillside Road. The ACL was evidently hoping that Dolgarrog would become recognised as a model

The first ACL houses – Croft Cottages 1911

industrial village after the style of Lord Leverhulme's Port Sunlight development. However, after the first 20 'model cottages' had been built, the subsequent developments consisted of less attractive houses of wood and corrugated iron construction.

In 1913 two larger houses were built for managers. In fact managers and heads of departments were encouraged or even required to live in the village and take a leading part

Plas Rhaiadr, the Works Manager's house

The Plas Rhaiadr Temperance Hotel

in its social life. Also a house, the Aviary, was built to accommodate the works cashier and his collection of Canaries! Should a member of management complain that there was nowhere to live, quite quickly the ACL would put up a house or bungalow for him and issue instructions to move in forthwith!

The Plas Rhaiadr Temperance Hotel which served as the Manager's Club, quite austere!

The Board tried to have the licence transferred from the Newborough Arms, which they owned at the southern edge of the village, to the old Plas Rhaiadr Hotel. This failed so they renamed it 'The Dolgarrog Temperance Hotel' and it was run by the works secretary who lived in the building. Its interiors were rather drab, even grim one might say! It was leased to the British Legion in 1927.

Religion

In 1913 Dolgarrog was designated as a conventional district for the ecclesiastical parish of Llanbedr-y-Cennin and so was able to have its own church and resident curate. A simple wooden structure was built, dedicated to the Virgin Mary but the village never had a chapel.

In 1911 an English Band of Hope was established by J.R. Jones a Calvinist minister from nearby Tal-y-bont but it did not last, and it was only in 1920 that they were able to use the school building for a Sunday School and Band of Hope meetings. When the school was washed away in the flood

The first Dolgarrog Church

Interior of the church

they had to meet in various private houses until in it was able to move more permanently into the Aviary. By 1943 they had a membership of between seventy and eighty young people and held eleven classes each Sunday.

The Welsh Language

The main language of the area was naturally Welsh but by the time that this industrial development came to Dolgarrog English had begun to penetrate even those traditional Welsh communities. Almost certainly the bosses of the new enterprise were not gifted with the 'Language of Heaven'. Indeed the character of the village was of an English-speaking community with no roots in the area. In the factory the majority of workers were bi-lingual and those monoglot English workers seemed to be able to get along with fellow Welsh workers when they happened to revert to their native tongue.

The First World War

By 1914 there were around 200 men at the works and it

appeared that the ACL was flourishing, but in reality the factory was constantly operating at under capacity and there were problems with the water supply during the summer months.

The outbreak of war introduced new problems. Dolgarrog became a 'controlled establishment' under military guard against 'saboteurs and infernal machines'. All the workers were issued with 'Private' badges. By the summer of 1915 a quarter of the workforce had volunteered to go to war. The ACL made an allowance to their dependents, as did many other employers at this time.

The ACL benefited from an increased demand to support the war effort. This was fortunate, because previously a large part of their output had been exported to Germany. Difficulties with the supply of Bauxite from France soon became another problem. Fortunately the Company had a stock pile, which kept them in business. The French Government declared Bauxite to be contraband and the military authorities commandeered the ACL's warehouse at St Raphael. Not an action you might expect from a country we were fighting to defend! This, and the impossibility of chartering shipping meant that their stocks at Hebburn on Tyneside, dwindled alarmingly.

There was 'trouble at mill' as well because the remaining workers were at odds with the management, demanding shorter hours and better pay. A war bonus was added to their pay packets which brought a labourer's wage up to £3.1s.10d for a forty-eight hour week. Even so, things deteriorated as they were required to work longer and harder. A local branch of the Labourer's Union was set up in Trefriw, which set out to recruit the Dolgarrog workforce.

During the war, in 1916, a plant was installed to produce aluminium granules but there was an explosion which injured five workmen, one of whom subsequently died.

Alterations were made to make the process safe as this powder was needed for use in paint, explosives and incendiary bombs and was quite important to the war effort. Jack had a particular interest in this as he owned the patents to the process. From 1916 to 1919 the Company paid him royalties for the use of the patent.

Eleven men from the works were killed in the war including Harry Jack's only son, Lt. Henry Claude Jack who died in a plane crash.

The New Rail Link

In 1916 a standard gauge rail link was built connecting the works to a newly built station on the LNWR branch line on the other side of the river from Dolgarrog. A girder bridge was built and the line went into the works with sidings to all the departments. The Corporation owned and operated at least four steam shunting engines on the line. It proved to be a great benefit to the despatch department, and also to employees who lived away from the village as the Company arranged for a free passenger service to be operated on it.

The girder bridge over the Afon Conwy

The works train bringing workers from across the valley

Two very old passenger coaches were acquired and a service was arranged to pick up workmen arriving on the branch line at 7.30 a.m. for the day shift. Office staff arriving for their 9 a.m. start had to walk the mile or so to the works, but at knocking off time, 5.15 p.m. all were entitled to use it. The better of the two coaches was supposed to be for the office staff and there could be squabbles if a workman tried to sit in it! It is believed that the service continued until about 1932, but by the 1940's they had found a new role as changing huts for the swimming pool and football pitch. The one at the swimming pool had an interesting feature in that the compartment partition, which separated the men's from the women's section, did not reach the ceiling!

Despite the construction of the rail link the ACL continued to use lorries. A road was built alongside the rail siding across the valley, using the girder bridge to access the railway station. A fleet of vehicles was acquired: lorries, a van which doubled as an ambulance when needed, eleven Trojan tourer cars with solid tyres and one saloon model with pneumatic tyres for the use of Crossley Colley, the

The works garage for the fleet of cars

Construction Manager and to ferry potential investors and the directors from Llandudno Junction Station to Dolgarrog. These vehicles were looked after by a foreman and four chauffeurs. They also had an electric car that could do as much as 20 mph and which was used to transport some key workers from Trefriw, where they lived. The car was plugged into the power station to be charged up during the day – shades of green one might say!

In 1916 it was decided to end the use of water transport, so the wharf at the works and a number of the barges were broken up. The tramway which had been laid to the river was also taken up.

With the new rail link in place, work was able to start on a development to build a rolling mill. Up to this time the works had only produced ingots of aluminium which were sent elsewhere for rolling out into sheets. A new building was constructed housing four mills along with an annealing furnace and gas producer.

Water Shortages and New Dams

A continuing, major problem was the shortage of water. There were droughts in 1913 and 1915. A decision was made to take water from Afon Dulyn and channel it through a tunnel 1,440 yards long into Llyn Eigiau. This poject was started in 1914 and took two years to complete. This was not a cure but gave them breathing space. The ACL still needed to look for further improvements to its supply. The Board decided to proceed with a plan to increase the capacity of the Cowlyd Dam, along with a dam at Lyn Llugwy in the Nant Ffrancon Valley, to be connected by a leat to Cowlyd. So after agreement with the Water Board who owned Cowlyd, work was started to build a new dam wall 450 yards long and 50 ft high thus increasing the capacity to 3,110 million gallons, making it the deepest lake in Wales.

The Tramway to Cowlyd

Work was started on a tramway from the Dolgarrog incline head to Cowlyd and Ffynnon Llugwy and this was completed by August 1917. About a hundred Irish labourers were employed on the project. They were well known for their rowdy Saturday night drinking bouts in Dolgarrog, but they were hard workers. They were accommodated in tin huts behind Taylor Avenue, a place known to this day as 'Meany's' after Mrs Meany, wife of Will Meany (the ganger) who ran their canteen there, discreetly out sight from Plas Maenan across the valley, where Harry Jack had just taken up residence.

As soon as the tramway was completed Harry Jack arranged for representatives of the water supply board and senior members of the works staff to attend a sod cutting ceremony at the dam site. The party of twenty-four made their way to the incline from Dolgarrog, those who were fit or nervous made their way up on foot, only the sedentary or the rash braved the train on the incline. From the top of the incline a train of converted tipping wagons took them to Cowlyd. At the site Harry Jack produced a silver spade for for the cutting of the first sod. Afterwards Jack entertained them to dinner at the Porth Llwyd Hotel.

The Directors visit the Eigiau construction site

The work was started with the Irishmen digging out the foundations but somehow the work slipped and by May 1918 there were only about seventy still at work and of those only ten were actually digging the dam, while the others were employed repairing the tramway – which might indicate that it had been shoddily built in the first place. The Board had an idea to use prisoners of war under contract and to house them in the Eigiau Valley. However when the Board applied to the Ministry of Munitions they were told that prisoners could not be used on construction work in the winter, but to try again in the spring. However, by then the war was over and they had been shipped back to their own countries. Before much more work was done on the dam the

North Wales Power and Traction Company, the owners of the Cwm Dyli Power Station found that there was not enough demand for their electricity. So in 1918 they were negotiating for, in effect, a take over by the ACL which took a controlling interest. Harry Jack now became the Managing Director of both companies. He saw this move as strengthening his own power and influence.

Chapter 5

Visions of a Garden City

In 1919 Dolgarrog became a Civil Parish in its own right. This added to Harry Jack's power base, as predictably he was elected Chairman. This was useful in that the ACL was able to demand facilities from the County Council such as a school – which was established in the old Territorial Army hut near the works and was very successful. However the Council did turn down ACL's request for a resident village bobby!

Social Life

Meanwhile, generous leisure facilities were being built for the workmen and their families: a children's playground, a rifle range for the works shooting club, tennis courts and a men's institute for the lower orders. This was housed in a

The Working Men's Institute library

The billiard room of the Working Men's Institute later to become the village church after the flood

former farm and outbuildings, converted on the cheap. But it had a billiards room, a primitive library and an American Bowling Alley.

A workmen's Co-op was built on the main road opposite the factory run by the ACL. Supplies of butter, eggs and milk

The Working Men's clubroom with central heating!

The village shops

surplus to the requirements of the Managing Director at Plas Jack, were collected by pony-drawn milk-float to be delivered to the shop to be sold. Cash sales from this arrangement were paid to the works clerk who also carried out stock checks at the other company owned businesses: the Bedol Inn at Tal-y-bont and the Newborough Arms. In 1922 the Co-op was taken over by E. B. Jones, a well known north Wales Grocery chain. The building is still there to this day. Other shops were added over the years.

By 1918 an elaborate Assembly Room had been built, it had a large stage flanked by portraits of the King and Queen and lavish scenery for entertainments and film shows, as well as an excellent dance floor. A football pitch was built nearby, and in 1919 a swimming pool behind the Works. A Social Council was set up to co-ordinate the workers and their families spare time activities, and they were encouraged to use the facilities. There were amateur dramatics, glee parties, a pierrot troupe, sports days and an annual carnival. A 'Bulletin' was published from 1918 onwards, a bit like a gossip magazine with near the bone

Abden Clee houses being built, with the Assembly Rooms and Bankfield House behind

The local football team

Llyn Cowlyd

Cowlyd Dam wall

Coedty Dam as it is today

The hydro pipeline from the Coedty Dam

The hydro pipelines at Dolgarrog today

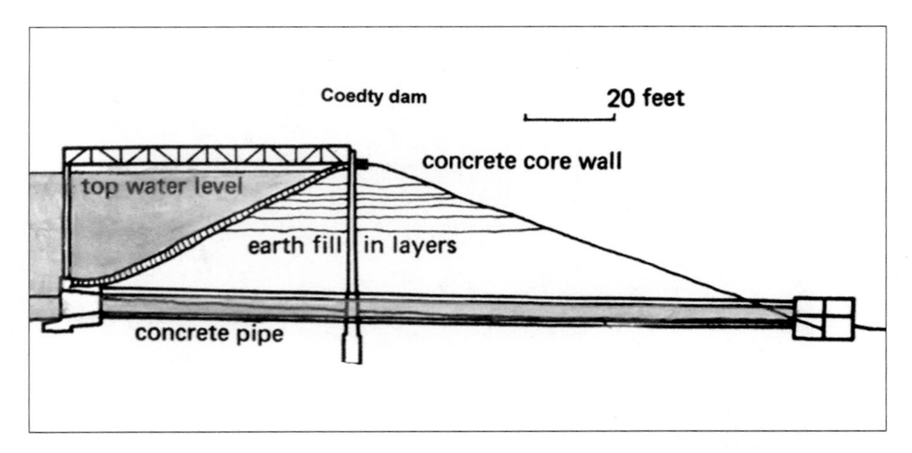

Section of Coedty Dam showing its construction

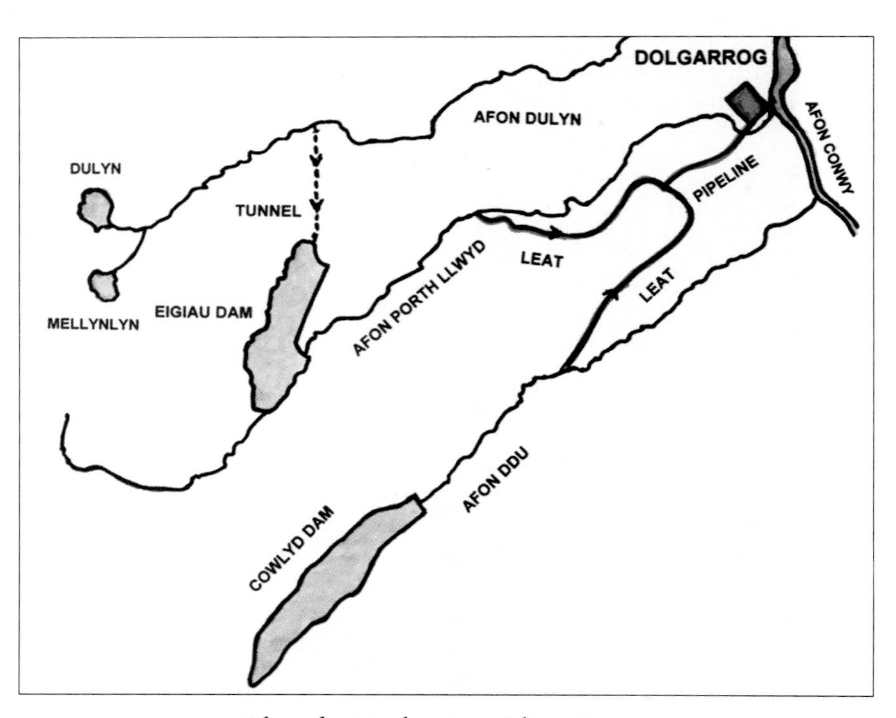

Plan of original water catchment area

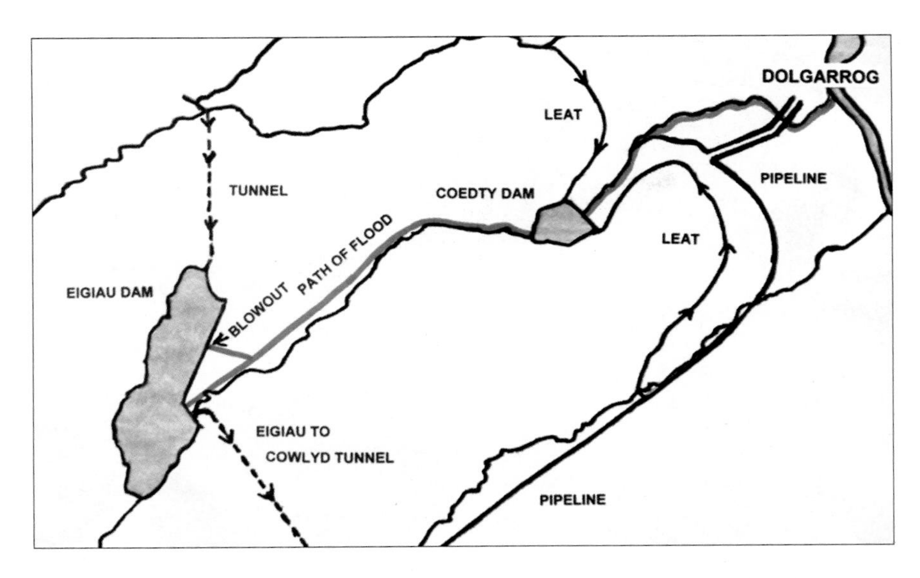

Plan of catchment area after disaster showing the track of flood waters

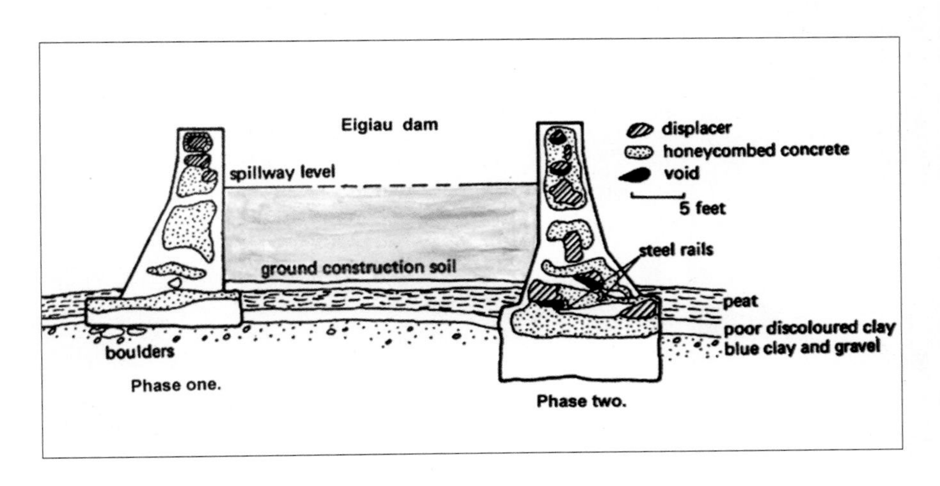

Section drawing of Eigiau Dam walls

The War Memorial gardens

Interior, the new Assembly Hall

Plas Jack, the terrace 1

Plas Jack, the terrace 2

The external entrance to the tunnel into Plas Maenan

The inner entrance gate

The new owner of Plas Maenan, Mark Richards, in the tunnel

The strongroom door

The Church Bell – recovered after the disaster

The children's Song Book saved from the wreckage of the school by a teacher

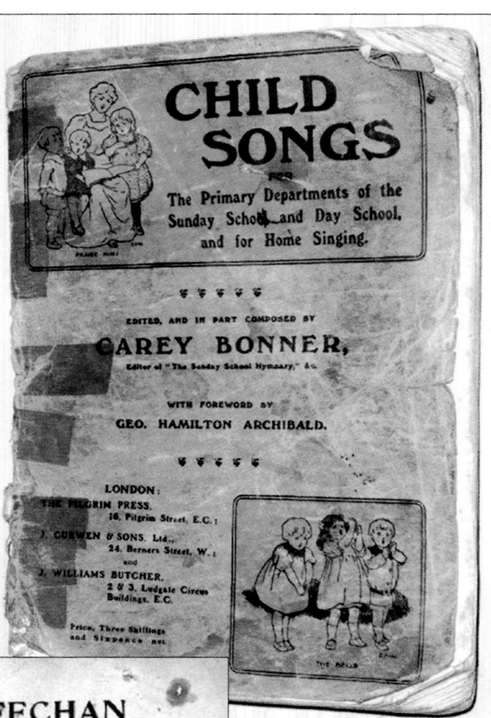

LLANFAIRFECHAN

TOWN HALL CINEMA.

Thursday, Friday & Saturday

NOVEMBER 5th, 6th, & 7th. 1925

The Management have at great expense secured

THE FIRST COPY

OF THE

Dolgarrog

CATASTROPHE.

NIGHTLY AT 7.30

MATINEE: SATURDAY AT 2.30.

NO INCREASE IN PRICES.

Caxton Press, Llanfairfechan.

A poster for a newsreel film of the disaster showing in the Assembly Rooms just three days later

The locomotive, Eigiau, *now restored*

The entrance to the new Boulder Walk

The Memorial to the dead

The walkway through the boulders

The author surveys some of the giant boulders

Hydro electric generators in the power house

The Tyddyn farm which was the Working Men's Institute and later the village church after the disaster

The new surfing lake built by Surf Snowdonia

An expert surfer shows his skills at Surf Snowdonia

Some of the girls who worked at the factory

jokes and sly digs at anyone who was out of favour with the editor. There was something for everyone, men and women alike. By now women were taking a much larger part in the community life and many actually worked in the factory. There were lectures and discussions on important topics at which Harry Jack would turn up, on at least one occasion he contributed his own opinion which turned it into almost a lecture by itself!

The Bulletin

Something of the social history of this community can be found in the reports in *The Bulletin* such as the Victory Celebrations in July 1919. Victory Celebrations started with a fancy dress ball in the Assembly Rooms, Harry Jack was dressed to kill as a Red Cross Knight. Next day the procession assembled at Dolgarrog Bridge, every available horse-driven and self-propelled vehicle was pressed into service, including a traction-engine which ran off the road near the Newborough Arms. There was a band and a

The 1919 Victory Parade

number of floats including one displaying an effigy of the Kaiser complete with executioner. The fancy dress costumes represented Carolina Minstrels, King John signing the Magna Carta, Medieval knights, nurses, pirates and soldiers, amongst others. When the procession reached Tal-y-bont the Kaiser was beheaded! In the evening Harry Jack's house was ceremoniously floodlit. By now the house had in own electricity supply direct (by overhead cables across the valley) from the works power station! I bet he never paid an electricity bill!

Fancy dress seems to have been very popular in Dolgarrog: when the Cowlyd Dam was opened a fancy dress ball was held in the Assembly Rooms. The dresses ranged from a Restoration Courtier (Mrs Jack), a Circassian Princess (Mrs Bradbrook), a lady of the harem (Mrs Pettifer), Autumn (Miss Bates), Night (a girl from Blaenau Ffestiniog), a Colleen, a Dutch girl, and Goody Two Shoes to General Knowledge – whatever that was!

The end of the 1919 Victory Parade at Tal-y-Bont

Harry Jack's Work Ethic

The ethic was: give the workers decent accommodation and leisure facilities along with regular and comparatively well paid employment, and they will co-operate with management. In Harry Jack's own words:

> we know that rendering our people happy is our best policy, and our people know that making our concern prosperous is in their own best interests.

In fact the workers were quite happy to go along with this. They were for a large part Anglo-Scottish and English speaking and took reassurance from the paternalistic attitude of Harry Jack and the Company.

Accommodation

At this time there were about 600 workers on the payroll. The Company had had a very good war and created a successful and dynamic community, but the problem of accommodation had become acute. The village was full to bursting: with only sixty-seven separate dwellings, including the farms, the parish was the most crowded in the county. Many families took in lodgers, and many of the young women lodged at 'The Sillans', near to the works, surrounded by thick hedges and watched over by a formidable matron!

One little story is about Sarah Grace Williams who is mentioned later on. She was born at Coedty Farm, where the dam is to-day, and lived with her parents there. She had to attend the school at Tal-y-bont and clearly it was not an option for her to walk to school every day. It is a climb of nearly 1,000 ft up a narrow winding road so she stayed with her grandmother, during the week, at Hednant Cottage above Porth Llwyd. The coal supplies came to a coal yard next to the factory by steam train. Dick, the engine driver gave a signal with his whistle to tell her grandmother that the coal was in. She would then go down and pick up a one hundredweight bag of coal on her back and carry it all the way home – which was several hundred feet up from the valley floor. She lived to the ripe old age of eighty-six and is buried at Tal-y-bont Chapel.

As early as 1918 a decision had been taken to build a Garden City including an hotel and several shops in the village. It was to provide accomodation for the 400 to 500 men who worked for the company. However no start on this project was made until 1922 when a contract was let to McAlpine's for the ground work. This involved the opening up of a substantial quarry to the south of Porth Llwyd Falls. This had crushing and screening machinery connected by a 3 ft gauge railway line and used several steam locomotives to take the excavated stone to be used in the building of the foundations, roads and terraces, on the hillside above the works. This quarry, much later, became the unofficial adventure playground for the village kids.

The Abden Clee houses

The main road was straightened and a bridge built over the incline to replace what had been a very hazardous level crossing. This work was completed by late 1924 and a contract was awarded to the Abdon Clee Stone Quarry Company of Shropshire for 100 of their own design, pre-fabricated concrete, semi-detached houses. The total cost was £50,336 plus £12,177 for the drains and roads – that's £625 each – quite a bargain! These are the houses you can still see to-day on the main road through the village.

The names of the new roads were connected to ACL. The Chairman gave his name: Clark to the street connecting High Street to Station Road. Bibby Road and Taylor Avenue were named after ACL directors. Samuel Bibby was a member of the family that founded and owned the world renowned Bibby Shipping Line. He lived in nearby Rowen in a house called Plas-yn-Roe which was later to become the home of the famous television presenter Jess Yates. And Graham Road was named after one of the Company's solicitors.

One of the Abden Clee houses with an upstairs flat

This was one of the largest housing developments in Wales at the time and there have been no major developments of the village since. However, the timber and corrugated iron bungalows which were common until after WW2 have all been replaced with conventional brick and slate houses.

The first house was finished by Autumn 1925, and let at a rent of 12/6d a week for the non-parlour design. There wasn't a rush to occupy them and many remained empty for a long time. The reason: the rent on the old cottages was 2/6d per week and the canny villagers weren't in a hurry to splash out on such extravagant living! Some of the houses had to be adapted to flats with an external wooden staircase to one of the three bedrooms. In an effort to fill the houses ACL decreed that any new employee must live in a company house. This was not popular! Initially the electricity came at a fixed charge, but when it was observed that every window was blazing away in the evenings the ACL started charging by the unit. In fact Dolgarrog was known as 'Piccadilly Circus' to the other residents of the Conwy Valley as it also had electric street lights, probably the first in north Wales.

Plas Jack

In 1914 the ACL bought the large house, Plas Maenan, on the opposite side of the valley for the princely sum of £5,500 and shortly afterwards the Board accepted an offer from the Managing Director to rent it for £75 per year. Harry Jack then moved in with his wife, and sister-in-law and her husband – who was the stores superintendent at the works. Fancying himself as part of the landed gentry, Harry Jack changed the name of the house to Maenan Manor. There is no record of him ever having paid the rent and bearing in mind that his remuneration was £2,000 a year, one might say that he was a bit cheeky!

To the Welsh speaking community the house was known as 'Plas Jack'! Employees were not welcome except at Christmas when the village children were invited over for a

Plas Maenan, known locally as Plas Jack

party. The only regular visitors were a group of up to twenty men from the works who were employed on what was officially listed as 'Maenan Alterations'. Harry Jack apparently did not inform his fellow directors just what the works were. The first alteration was a new drive leading down to the new Dolgarrog Station. Next, and this was a major undertaking, the building of the vast new terrace in front of the house which dominates it to this day. This must have used thousands of tons of rock and hundreds of tons of sand and cement, plus hundreds of man hours to build. To achieve this a quarry was opened up nearby, complete with a tramway down to the main road where the rocks were loaded onto steam trucks to be transported up to Plas Jack.

One very interesting feature of this terrace is that a substantial tunnel was built underneath it, giving easy and discreet access to the cellars of the house. Finally a driveway towards the Maenan Abbey was started, but never completed. How Harry Jack managed to keep all this work hidden from his directors is somewhat of a mystery! It may be that since the directors were mostly investors in the ACL the attitude was that so long as the profits rolled in they were not disposed to ask any awkward questions. But the workmen were warned that should any of the directors appear unexpectedly, they should make themselves scarce!

Harry Jack lived well, and entertained lavishly when he wished to charm and impress potential investors in some of his ambitious schemes. Plas Jack was a perfect stage, with its commanding views of the valley below, for Harry Jack to strut his stuff. In fact he was given an entertainments allowance of £500 a year – at a time when one could get a good meal at a Llandudno hotel for 10/- (50p)! To his workers he was something of a martinet and was viewed with awe, whilst being liked and respected by members of the works hierarchy.

Chapter 6

Dam and Empire Building

Electricity Commissioners Inquiry

Harry Jack saw Dolgarrog being in a position to dominate the commercial future of north Wales. The war had shown up the weaknesses in the power supply industry and in 1919 the Government set up an advisory body – the Electricity Commissioners who were tasked with reviewing the organisation of the industry, which at the time was very fragmented.

In 1920 they held an inquiry to look at the situation in north Wales and south Cheshire. They had to choose between two schemes: one from the Chester Corporation, the other from the North Wales Power Traction Company which had proposed improvements at Dolgarrog and Cwm Dyli hydro electric station on the slopes of Snowdon in the Maentwrog Valley.

Needless to say, Harry Jack and the NWPTC won the day. It meant that he came in time, to control the electricity supplies to the whole of north Wales including the industrial areas of Wrexham and as far as the railway works at Crewe. The Maentwrog Hydro Electric Power Station using Trawsfynydd Lake was operational by 1928.

By 1919, with expanded production at Dolgarrog, a number of maintenance departments were set up to look after the factory and the estate. An engineering workshop was equipped to deal with most of the day to day demands of the works. Fitters were recruited from north Wales quarries so that the works became quite self reliant. A saw mill was established, and a workforce of carpenters, bricklayers, plumbers, plasterers and painters. This no doubt provided Harry Jack the perfect wherewithal to do his 'Plas Maenan' improvements. The works Construction Manager, Crossley Colley, must have been party to the arrangements but one can only assume that he could claim the he was:

only obeying orders!

Going back to 1918, work on the Llugwy Dam, in the Ogwen Valley, had been completed but work on a leat to Cowlyd and on the dam itself had ground to a halt. The reasons are lost in the mists of time! In 1923 contracts were exchanged with McAlpines to complete the work and also to build a tunnel from Eigiau to Cowlyd, and a leat from Afon Ddu to a new dam to be built at Coedty – all designed by Ralph Freeman who had by now become a partner with Sir Douglas Fox and Partners. He was by now forty-three and well versed in his trade, or so you might expect! A 6 ft diameter pipeline was to be built from Coedty to Dolgarrog where a new power station was to be built next to the old one.

A leat that fed water into the Coedty Dam

Ralph Freeman, architect of the dams

Upwards of 300 navvies lived at Cowlyd in the usual shanty town where a grocery shop was provided for them. Most were Irish, but some were locals from Bethesda and they made their way on foot over Tal-y-braich to the site. On Saturdays the Irishmen would descend on Llanrwst to buy their groceries, paying young local lads to look after their purchases while they attended the pubs. They were renowned for their rowdyness and spent Saturday nights sleeping under hedges and in house doorways in Dolgarrog, much to the disgust and fear of the female residents. On Sundays they returned to the work camp nursing their hangovers!

The twin pipes feeding the power station

In 1919 there was a shortage of cement which brought everything to a halt for five months. By November the dam was up to 20 ft above foundations and was not completed until November in 1921. It had a capacity of 3,100 million gallons and became the deepest man made lake in Wales. The construction was of a concrete membrane probably about 3 ft thick, with a soil embankment each side, the inner side being encased in a stone layer to prevent erosion. Its total length was 450 yards and the height above ground level 50 ft.

The Opening of Cowlyd Dam

The official opening of the site was held on the morning of 20 September 1922. The guests were hauled up the incline from Dolgarrog in trucks, described by some as: a nerve racking experience. They were then taken on to the dam by train. Sir John Snell, Chairman of the Electricity Commissioners, performed the official opening by drinking water from the dam from an Elizabethan goblet. In his speech he looked forward to the day when the Chester to Holyhead Railway line would be electrified, farsighted one might say! Replying, Harry Jack said it was important to conserve fossil fuels – that the South Wales Coalfield would be seriously depleted in sixty years time:

> If the work of developing the natural resources of the country was put in hand at once, they could provide work for many of those that had fought for their country and were tired of living off doles.

On their return to Dolgarrog a luncheon was held in the Assembly Rooms 'transformed into the semblance of an Eastern Tent'. Entertainment was provided by local artistes and the works orchestra. In the evening there was a costume ball.

Takeovers and New Schemes

In the spring of 1921 the ACL bought all the ordinary shares of The North Wales Power & Traction Company and their

The old entrance to the factory

subsidiary The Porthmadoc, Beddgelert & South Snowdon Railway Company for a total of £10. In so doing, Harry Jack became both the Official Receiver and a Director of the Company.

As the result of a number of take-overs and amalgamations Harry Jack came to control all the north Wales narrow gauge railways as well as the Snowdon Mountain Railway. Included were the Snowdon Summit Hotel and the Royal Victoria Hotel in Llanberis.

Dolgarrog became the centre for renewed railway mania, this time for narrow gauge railways. In fact Harry Jack even had an idea to build a second rack Mountain Railway up Snowdon from Rhyd Ddu, on the other side of the mountain from Llanberis and planned to electrify the Snowdon Mountain Railway and make it dual track.

Big Schemes for North Wales Narrow Gauge Railways

In 1921 at an Enquiry by the Light Railway Commission an order was granted for the Welsh Highland Railway, which was formed by the amalgamation of the Porthmadoc,

Beddgelert & South Snowdon Railway Company and the North Wales Narrow Gauge Railway to complete the physical connection between the Welsh Highland Railway at Beddgelert and the Ffestiniog Railway at Porthmadoc, using the track bed of the failed South Snowdon Railway Company. The connection was completed in 1923 which meant that it was then possible to travel by narrow gauge all the way from outside Caernarfon to Blaenau Ffestiniog. This connection has only now, ninety odd years later, been restored with an extension from central Caernarfon – a distance of forty miles.

At this time these railways were still carrying a substantial though declining volume of slate traffic, but Harry Jack's predictions for passenger traffic were by now being undermined by the bus companys taking away many potential local passengers.

Despite efforts to drum up tourist traffic results were disappointing. At a stormy meeting at the North Wales Power & Traction Company's offices in Dolgarrog in November 1924 Harry Jack was forced to resign his

The factory in 1925 before the disaster

Chairmanship of both Companies. He remained on the Board until the following year and retained a shareholding in the Welsh Highland Railway up til his death. In fact when the enthusiasts came to restoring the Welsh Highland Railway they had to buy Harry Jack's shares from his living relatives in Canada before they could proceed.

This was the first crack in the success story, which might have indicated his management style was not the best suited for some operations – such as the complexity of running railways.

The New Coedty Dam and Power Station

The new Coedty Dam and Power Station were completed in the summer of 1924 but there were problems from the start. On test one of the pipeline joints failed and the consequent flood damaged the Plas Rhaiadr Hotel and the shops in Dolgarrog. Fortunately a quick witted McAlpine's chargehand managed to turn off the flow before serious damage could occur. The leat to Afon Ddu was completed, but there was a delay in starting the tunnel designed to take water from Eigiau to Cowlyd and this was not completed until 1928.

Chapter 7

Disaster strikes

The Dam Breaks

The night watchman Albert Jones ('Bert Lake') at the dam site did not realise the significance of the event until 9 pm at which time he rang the time office in the factory, and was told to hang on as the supervisor was on another line. Albert received an electric shock from the phone, so it was reported. He made his way to the Cowlyd Dam – about four miles away over the mountain to try to raise the alarm from the phone there but by then it was too late. This is the story reported in the press at the time – which I believe was planted deliberately by the management.

There is absolutely no doubt that if a warning had been given promptly then no lives would have been lost.

At 9.10 pm Mary Griffiths, wife of the manager of the Porth Llwyd Hotel in the village, phoned the time office at the works when she saw water flooding across the main road. A few minutes later she rang again to say that a part of the hotel annexe had been swept away. Realising that there was serious danger she, with her husband and two maids, Miss Sinott and Miss Alice Owen, up to their armpits in flood water, climbed to safety over the Cowlyd Pipeline Bridge assisted by two boy scouts Thomas Meany and Charles Carpenter.

The breach at Eigiau while it looks dramatic now, would actually only have caused bad flooding in Dolgarrog had it not been for the recently completed Coedty Dam right in the path of the torrent pouring from Eigiau. Coedty quickly overflowed – it's spillway not able to cope, and this caused the collapse of the wall which almost instantly released a violent flood of seventy-five million gallons of water, taking with it an avalanche of boulders, weighing up to 500 tons each, roaring down the gorge to reach the village below at some time shortly after 9.30 pm.

Another eyewitness report says that at 9.30 a low rumble was heard from the top of the hill which gave a general warning, and the frightened villagers made a dash for their lives to the higher ground and safety.

The alarm was given by the Rev. William Evans, the Curate who, realising the significance of the noise coming from the hills above the village, ran through Porth Llwyd shouting a warning to people, while others joined in the cry.

Mrs Maggie Allen, of Tal-y-bont, recalled that she and her parents heard a tremendous explosion and then a

The Revd. William Evans, Curate (centre) one of the many heroes of the event

thunderous roar coming from the hill above Dolgarrog. Her father went to the brow of the hill til he could see the village. The sight before him, even in the darkness, was a sea of black water everywhere. He was terrified by what he saw and completely shaken by it so she says. This was a man not prone to showing his emotions. The family had relations in Dolgarrog who fortunately survived.

Most of the villagers were enjoying a film show in the Assembly Rooms. A Mr Watson and his family from Llanrwst used to come every Tuesday and Friday night to show silent films. A night at the flicks was very popular in those days before television, and a large part of the population of the village were at the show on the fateful night. Someone from the works went across the road to No.1 Croft Cottages where twenty year old Sarah Grace Williams lived with her parents (she worked as a secretary in the factory) and asked her to go and warn the cinema manager to tell the patrons not to go home because of the flooding. When she delivered her message the manager said to her:

> don't be so daft you silly girl.

He must have relented because he did warn the patrons. They filed out and were able stay safely on high ground watching the disaster unfold before them. Some of the men went to help with the rescues. Fortunately there was a bright moon which helped them. In the event Sarah was not able to get home because of the floods and had to stay at a friends house.

Fourteen year old Fred Brown was at the show with his siblings, twin brothers Douglas and Glyn, sister Beatrice and other brothers Gilbert and John. His mother Elizabeth and father William were at their home, No.1 The Bungalows, in Porth Llwyd when the torrent struck. His sister Elizabeth, aged sixteen, would spend the night in the old school building – she survived by clambering onto the roof and was picked up later by her father who had also clambered his way to safety. Mrs Brown and her four year old daughter Bertha did not survive. Fred told of hearing the church bell ringing as the church was swept away. At daybreak Fred set off on his bike to try to find his mother. He cycled across the Dolgarrog girder bridge, down the valley to Tal-y-cafn then back up the valley to Ty'n-y-groes then Tal-y-bont in a fruitless search of all the farms for her.

Many refugees from the flood were accommodated in the Assembly Hall and Bankfield House. The community rallied round and brought mattresses and blankets for them to bed down for the night. Others who were in their houses at the foot of the gorge had little chance as the wall of water, which a witness described as 50 ft high by 50 ft wide, crashed down upon them.

In the works

Nineteen year old Thomas Jervis of Tal-y-bont was a worker in the rolling mill. He had joined the workforce in 1922 and from 1923 helped to build the new Abdon Clee houses until March 1925 when he went back into the works. He had been on day shifts until the date of the disaster when he was put on the twelve hour nightshift starting at 6 pm. There were about 110 men working the rolling mill and fifty or so in the casting and furnace room, when at about 9 pm the lights went out apart from some emergency lighting. (The timing is at odds with other witnesses but the power failure may have been localised in the works just cutting off the rolling mill). A big cheer went up from the workers as this meant they could have a break from the very heavy work of the manipulating the aluminium ingots. Soon they noticed that a trickle of water was seeping in under the corrugated iron walls of the building. Then the walls were being pushed in by the force of the water. As they had not been alerted they did not realise the danger they were in.

The normal course of the river at this time actually went right through the middle of the works. Then mud and stones started to flood in. Rather than get out immediately they set to, conscientiously, to oiling the rollers so that they would not rust! Only when the water was rising so fast that one of the men said:

> I am not staying here anymore

did they make their way to the highest point of the shed, where they broke a window to get out and had to wade through the water to higher ground. They stood and watched, horrified, as the flood, which was described as being like Niagara Falls, engulfed the village. They stayed there till daylight which revealed the valley was just a vast lake as far as the eye could see and there was a huge canyon with a mountain of massive boulders below it where the village had been. They were then told to go home and come back at 6 pm to clear the mud from the power house as there was an urgent need to get the generators back on.

> The road was thronged with villagers fleeing before the flood which they could hear but not see, recalled one survivor. Then it came down on us with a roar. The foam seemed to give the darkness a kind of ghostly light in which little incidents stood out. I saw mothers grabbing their children, I saw old men and a woman urging each other to hurry. I saw the land-lady and the two maids from the local hotel being carried away by rescuers, sometimes up to their armpits in water and I can never forget the awful crash when the torrent hit the bridge

over the stream. It was just brushed it aside like matchwood.

The Furnace Room

The power house was the first to be affected and sweeping on, the flood entered the furnace room. One by one the smelting pots exploded in great clouds of steam. The noise of the explosions and the steam added terror to the distraught inhabitants of the village. The chargeman, Morris Morgan, said that with three others he was imprisoned for seven hours:

> We were in pitched darkness and the water was up to our waists. From time to time the furnaces exploded throwing metal all over us. We stayed motionless for fear of being engulfed. Eventually the rescue party got us out with ropes.

The re-casting department

Gallant Rescue Work

The Rev. William Evans went breast high into the water as he struggled to free men trapped in the power house. Recounting his own version of what he had witnessed and experienced after the dam broke provided a grim but thrilling narrative:

> I was on my way to the village when I heard a rumbling on the mountain. Concluding that something had gone wrong with the dam, I rushed to the old part of the village shouting to the inhabitants to get clear. I managed to escape the wave of water that struck to organise a small party of rescuers. We had reason to believe that four men were imprisoned in the works. There were six or seven of us tied together with a rope, with only a bicycle lamp for a light which James Hunter, the superintendant of the power house used, held above his head. We were up to our shoulders in water and every now and then one of us stumbled and had to be dragged up by rope. Among the

The bungalow, home of Works Timekeeper, a Mr Jones, washed away after he rescued his wife and child

> brave fellows who helped was Mr Sergeant Thomas, the works timekeeper. We managed at last to reach the four trapped men and succeeded in getting them away after working most of the night. One of the men said he had been trapped for seven hours.

Mr L.V.Lurring, Superintendant of the power house was on duty and the inrush of water was so sudden that he could not escape and for six hours – he was imprisoned with water up to his waist.

How the occupants of the village met their fates will probably never be known. It has been stated that the cries for help were heard but owing to the raging torrent it was impossible to get near them.

In one remarkable escape, time keeper Jones was on his way home from work when he heard the onrushing water. He was just in time to get his wife and child to safety when the flood struck his house – which was a wooden bungalow and carried it a distance of sixty or seventy yards, then it turned completely around and came to rest near a huge tree.

Mr Willie Williams with his wife and two young children were in their home, Hendy Farm, when they heard a terrible noise and found that the waters were invading their house. His first thoughts were to let the cows out but his wife said:

> no get the kids first.

They ran upstairs picking a up baby each and ran out to safety just in time. They watched their cows being swept away. Then they made their way to his father's house the adjoining farm, Tyn-y-Felin. Leaving his family there he made his way back to try to save what he could from his home. He found that a corner of the building had been washed away by the torrent. He later said that he had lost one of the finest meadows in the valley which now lay beneath an avalanche of mud and stones. Four cows, two calves and some pigs and chickens had also been swept away. The cows had somehow got ashore with the pigs and were now peacefully grazing, none the worse for their stormy experience. The calves did not survive. The family lost everything except a large brass cooking pot, the sort you make jam in – which is still in the family.

This is the account by Mr William Brown, which he gave to the inquest on his wife Elizabeth and three year old daughter Betty who were drowned. He described how he and his eight year old daughter Nellie had escaped when the alarm was given:

> My family and I were sitting in the house. We heard a terrible rumble from the top of the hill and when I got to the door I heard people shouting the dam had burst. Water was coming down the road and into the garden with great force. I thought perhaps there had been a break in the leat at the top of the cliff whence the water runs to the top of the pipeline as such as had occurred a fortnight earlier when it flowed along the road but was not so deep as now. (Note here that this is the first and only time that a recent previous flood in the village has been mentioned). I went next door to warn the MacDonalds but found no-body in there except a lodger. I then heard somebody shouting. It was Mrs Sinnott calling from her yard at Porthlwyd Cottage. I went to her and found her in the yard with her daughter Mrs Mackenzie and the little girl Mona. I helped them over into our garden – they were up to their waists in water there and they went up to MacDonalds bungalow. By this time my wife was out in our garden and my daughter Margaret was also there. My wife went in, wrapped a coat

around our other little girl, Betty (the deceased) and brought her out. I took Betty in my arms and ran with her up to the MacDonalds bungalow. The water was then coming over the wall. I thought my wife was following me. I got to the MacDonalds bungalow and just then I heard my own bungalow being swept away. I did not see my wife again. In the MacDonalds bungalow were Mrs McKenzie, Mona McKenzie and my daughter standing on a mat together. I had not got there a minute when we were swept away by the water. Something must have struck me because I do not remember anything more until I found myself in the flood near the second standard from the works of the overhead electricity transmission line. At the moment that I last remember anything, I had my child Betty in my arms and the bungalow was moving. I next found myself with the child, twenty or thirty yards from the electric standard which I managed to reach and climb up. How long I was clinging to the standard I have no idea but I got down after a time. I saw

Elizabeth Brown with her family, she died as did her daughter Betty

> my daughter Margaret at 7 am the following morning. She had escaped by clinging to the top of the wooden schoolhouse which had been washed about half a mile in the direction of the river. The standard was about 300 yds from the MacDonalds bungalow.

His daughter, eight year old Nellie gave her story, she said:

> As soon as I got out of the house I saw a big wave coming down on top of me, I had no time to do anything. I was swept down the valley and on the water, I must have been badly bruised because I passed out. When I came to I saw a bit of high land which I was able to climb onto and there I discovered a building. I took it at first to be one of the bungalows, but found it was the village school, part of which had been swept away. I crept into it and stayed there all night till I was found next morning.

William Jones, known to his workmates as 'Will Doctor' climbed onto the roof of the carbon plant and was stuck til the morning.

Among the dead were three members of the Sinnott family of Porth Llwyd Cottage. They had decided to leave Dolgarrog to live in another part of Wales. Seven days before their scheduled departure the flood swept them to their deaths. Mrs Sinnott, her daughter and granddaughter were killed but the house itself survived the torrent. When rescuers forced their way into the house they founds the Sinnott's dog crouched unharmed on a bed upstairs.

The Eigiau Tunnel Workmen

There was fear that eleven Irish navvies who were working on the Eigiau to Cowlyd tunnel might have been drowned. Later it was established that they had survived. Sadly a week

Spectators viewing damaged Porth Llwyd Cottage, home of the Sinnotts who died. Their dog survived upstairs. The policeman is almost certainly PC Jones of Tal-y-bont.

later one of the men was killed and four injured in a serious accident in the tunnel during blasting operations. Because the road up to Eigiau had been washed away it was impossible to get an ambulance to them, so the injured men were kept in a hut by the lakeside with an ambulanceman in charge overnight. At daylight the following day it took twenty-four men two hours to carry them over the streams and gullies on stretchers. On arrival at the top of the mountain overlooking Dolgarrog they were conveyed down the steep slope on the miniature railway to the waiting ambulance. They eventually arrived at Llandudno Cottage Hospital about eighteen hours after the incident.

The Casualties

Bessie and Ceridwen Evans' bodies were found next day by fishermen, in the river near Conwy. One of them was floating on a mattress which she was clutching. Mrs Sinnott's body was the last to be found, ten months later, on a mud flat near Tal-y-cafn.

The death toll was as follows:

Stanley and Dorothy Taylor of 1 Machno Terrace, and their daughter Sylvia, aged eighteen months.

Mrs Williams of 2 Machno Terrace.

Harold Victor Williams, who lodged at 2 Machno Terrace.

Mrs Susan Evans of 3 Machno Terrace, and her daughters Ceridwen aged five, Bessie three, and Gwen four months.

Mrs Elizabeth Brown of No.1 Bungalow and her daughter Bertha (Betty) aged three.

Stanley and Dorothy Taylor – both died

Mrs Sinnott of Porth Llwyd Cottage, her daughter Mrs McKenzie of 2 Dolgarrog Cottages, and Mona, Mrs McKenzie's daughter aged five.

William and Jennie Twynham of Tai'r Felin.

Stanley Taylor was employed in the recasting department and had served in the Royal Engineers during the war. He was an Assistant Scout Master and members of his troop were responsible for some of the rescues.

Harold Victor Williams, aged 30, was from Sarn, Bryn Caled near Welshpool. He was a linesman and electrician with the Power Company and normally worked at

Porthmadog. He was due to marry a Porthmadog girl the following Saturday but was buried the same day at St John's Church where he had been a member. Adding to the pathos, he had in his pocket the certificate of his marriage banns which had been published at Caerhun Church.

Survivors

Mrs McKenzie's two sons had pleaded with her all day to be allowed to go to the cinema and she had finally agreed. She was waiting for them at her mother's house until the show ended. Both boys survived.

The first news of the of the disaster was only learnt about in Llanrwst when a number of lady clerks, who worked for the ACL, arrived at 10 pm in a van they had commandeered. They were having a dance in the Sillans Hostel when the flood hit. At 9-30 someone poked his head through a window and shouted that:

> the dam has burst.

The chemists laboratory later renamed The Sillans and used to accommodate female staff

Eigiau Dam wall breach

The Coedty Dam after the disaster

The flood flowing past the Plas Rhaiadr Temperance Hotel

They rushed out hatless and coatless down Clark Street until a warning voice told them to make for Llanrwst.

The news soon circulated and in a very few minutes almost all the cars in the town were out with the owners offering to put them at the disposal of the authorities. Llanrwst became a refugee centre with the cars bringing the survivors from Dolgarrog to find welcome accommodation with sympathetic residents

It's worth mentioning that three days before the disaster, several people in Llanrwst had independently mentioned having seen an apparition in the form of an angel in the clouds above Dolgarrog.

District in darkness

The electricity supply to Llandudno, Colwyn Bay and Conwy failed at about 9.30 pm. All the entertainment houses had to shut down and refund their customers money. By 11 pm Llandudno Council was able to turn on their auxiliary supply to light the town and run the tram cars.

The main road through the village after the flood

On the Tuesday supplies were again disrupted until 5 pm when the Dolgarrog engineers were able to connect a supply up to the power station at Cwm Dyli, while Colwyn Bay and Conwy were without power until Tuesday evening. At the popular dance in Colwyn Bay's Pier Pavilion, the dancers at first thought it was just a blown fuse and continued the dance by candlelight. A touch of humour was imparted when a male dancer suggested that they could get along very well without a light at all! Businesses were badly hit but the ironmongers did a roaring trade in oil lamps and candles!

An astonishing collection of odds and ends had been brought up by fishermen from the Conwy Estuary, eight miles from Dolgarrog. There were pathetic relics, among them childrens dolls and rubber balls together with clothing. Also two watches, field glasses, birth, death and marriage certificates in boxes, letters, a stethoscope, walking sticks, umbrellas, a minute book of the local British Legion,

Boulders that buried Porth Llwyd village during the flood

a Sam Brown belt and war medals, including military medals belonging to QMS W. Jones. All these were handed in to Conwy Police Station. Among the articles recovered on the Conwy Quay were a piano, a chest of drawers and the

Flood damaged Hendy Farm with Porth Llwyd Cottage in the background

Pipes and the flood after the disaster

fragments of the oak font from the little church. A steamer was chartered to return the items to Dolgarrog.

On 12 November a message of condolence was received from the King. Tens of thousands of visitors, from far and wide, came to see the destruction. Some souvenir hunters took little things away with them which ought to have been left for their owners – one had a letter written by a girl to her sweetheart – taken from one of the cottages as well as a silver spoon. It does raise questions about the morality of some people.

These curious sightseers were not appreciated by the residents who resented their presence – on the other hand there had been many who would have willingly contributed to any relief fund for the benefit of the homeless, and they expressed surprise that there have been no boxes in which they could drop their mite.

ACL had expressed their intention to shoulder all the responsibility of the disaster both material and otherwise and they did not wish for any relief fund to be started.

Chapter 8

The Aftermath

Board Meeting 4 November

Incredibly at a board meeting of the directors of ACL just two days later, on 4 November, there was not even a mention of the disaster. It was as though nothing had happened! This was the day before the first of the funerals which Jack almost certainly would have attended. And just two days later, on the Sunday, Jack was handing out medals to thirteen of those who had shown bravery during the disaster. One might conclude that if the directors had not authorised the medals then they must have been paid for personally by Jack.

Funerals

The first four funerals, just three days after the disaster

The area was inundated with sightseers and for a time the police put up a road block to stop anyone without a bona fide reason to visit the area. The first three funerals – for Mrs McKenzie, William Twynham and Mrs Williams were held early on the Friday morning to avoid sightseers. The cortege set off along Clark Street and Station Road to the Dengighshire side of the valley, then down to

Tal-y-cafn Bridge and to the churchyard at Caerhun. The mourners were met by many local clergymen of all denominations and the Bishop of Bangor officiated.

Other funerals were held the next day. Mrs Brown's in Caerhun, Betty and Ceridwen Evans' at Llangwstenin and Harold Higgins', whose wedding day it would have been, at Porthmadog.

After that visitors came and had picnics much to the disgust of the villagers, and there was quite a market in souvenir picture postcards of the disaster.

Ordinary General Meeting 10 November

The first mention of the event was on 10 November at an Ordinary General Meeting of ACL in London. The Chairman McKenzie Clark said that they all deplored the calamity and the directors greatly deplored the loss of life.

Directors and shareholders passed a resolution of condolence with the bereaved families. He said that prior to this calamity the company was well on the way to success and he believed they would pull through, adding that they were covered to a large extent by insurances.

Jack gave a very rambling account and blamed it on the extraordinary downfall of rain over the watershed which fed the Eigiau Dam.

Board Meeting 3 December

Only at a directors meeting, a month later on 3 December, was the first detailed reference to the events. Jack reported that work was going on to clear the tail race of the new power station. He said that it was very much blocked with debris and work was progressing to clear it and the works.

The chief electrical engineer submitted a report on the work of the power house staff on the occasion of the recent accident at Dolgarrog. (Notice how it has now become an accident!) It was read and noted with great interest by the directors.

A request by several insurance companies regarding third party claims was read and the directors decided to meet them at a later date.

A very important matter was the directors fees which it was agreed should be paid forthwith!

Then Jack got round to a full report on: The Disaster at Dolgarrog and Damage Caused by the Bursting of the Eigiau Dam. He explained that a weakness had been discovered in the foundations of a portion of the dam taken over from the liquidators of Bott and Stennett. The contractors had not gone down to the depth for which they had been contracted and this defective construction resulted in the accident. It was difficult to fix responsibility for the faulty construction after so long a period, as the defective work was done before the liquidation of the old company. The directors approved the employment of an independent consulting engineer so that they would have his advice before re-constructing the dam.

The Board resolved to place on record their high appreciation of the devotion to duty and valuable services rendered by the whole of the employees of the Company on the occasion of the recent disaster and the great effort to bring the works into active operation. Not to be left out the Board extended hearty congratulations to Jack, the managing director, for his able efforts in organising and directing this work.

Board Meeting 21 December

At the next board meeting on 21 December it was reported that a claim had been lodged by the farmer Mr W.J.Roberts of Panteg for £6,000. It was agreed to refer it to their solicitors and Jack suggested that the the amount should not exceed the value of the farm. Bearing in mind the farmer had lost his animals, his land which was now covered in boulders, and his livelihood, this does not tally with the pronouncements of Jack just after the disaster, that everyone would be compensated for their losses by the Corporation!

The Board had also received a letter from the Home Office that an inspection of all the dams, pipes and waterways should be carried out by a competent civil engineer. The board agreed to appoint Gibb and Partners.

Board Meeting 6 January

On 6 January 1926 at a board meeting Jack reported that a Caterpillar Steam Navvy had been deployed to clear the works of an estimated 100,000 tons of debris. This is now two months since the event, when Jack had claimed publicly that the works would be up and running again in a couple of weeks! He also reported that work was proceeding to rebuild the Coedty Dam and clear the tail race of the power house.

Re-building the Coedty Dam

With reference to the claim by the farmer, Mr W.J. Roberts, the board decided that as the Corporation needed to acquire the land, they would authorise Harry Jack and Alfred McAlpine to complete the matter on the best possible terms. In fact it took until Feburary to settle the claim and even then they had no choice but to pay the full £6,000.

Now the Corporation were having financial problems because the insurance companies would not pay out until the they had a sight of the Home Office report, and also the cost of the rebuilding of Coedty and possibly the Eigiau dams. As a result the Corporation had to go their bank to borrow £100,000 to tide them over.

The 1910 Leaks

In October 1910 Jack had visited Eigiau of which phase two was not yet complete, and reported that:

> water was finding its way under the foundations.

The next month a leak was discovered which Bott and Stennett repaired but which did not resolve the matter. There was correspondence between Jack, on behalf of the Board, and Douglas Fox, of Freeman Fox and Partners on 13 March 1911 pointing out that:

> the Board recognised that there might have been small leaks here and there, but the fact that there were such a large number of leaks, seemed to them to point to either want of efficient supervision, or the non-skilled method of putting in the material, and they therefore desired to be further informed on the matter.

The reply read:

> it would in our opinion, have been impossible without considerable extra cost to have secured an absolutely water tight dam constructed of concrete. The present structure has withstood, without any damage, very severe pressure and wind tests and we believe that by 'rendering' the inner faces to as lower a level as possible the leakage will be reduced to a negligible quantity. The materials used were of good standard quality and the work was continually and carefully supervised by your Resident Engineer, whose devotion to the interests of the Company has been most praiseworthy.

Jack replied by pointing out that Hugh Owen, the Resident Engineer, had in fact been under Fox's supervision and had reported to them. Nothing more was done about the matter but in 1911 a phone line was installed down to the works. This was probably necessary for the instruction of the lakes watchman with regard to the regulation of the water for the power house. It must be noted here that the same gang are back in business, Ralph Freeman, plus Bott & Stennett. Plus ca change!

Chapter 9

The Inquests

The Inquest

An inquest was called to identify the deceased and to ascertain the cause of death. However questions that are not asked can often be more important than those that are, as we shall see!

Opening an inquest on 4 November, at Dolgarrog, the Coroner for north Caernarfonshire, J. Pentir Williams, said that 'Dolgarrog had a floating population' a rather unfortunate turn of phrase! He went on to say that 'it was impossible to estimate the extent of the catastrophe in regard to human life'. After being shown the locations where bodies had been found he formally adjourned the inquest until 1 December at Conwy Town Hall.

At the adjourned inquest on five of the bodies there was no legal representation for any of the victims or families involved, nor were there any independent, i.e. without a vested interest, qualified witnesses. Jack was actually present but he was not called as a witness!

Quite clearly the coroner had been thoroughly briefed, as in his prologue to the inquest he stated that the whole thing turned on whether the dam was properly constructed and whether the foundations were properly laid. He even went on to suggest that the dam should have gone down to the rock for a sound foundation. As far as he understood it water had worked its way under the dam. After describing the dam he said that the water from the break had flowed down into another artificial dam, Coedty, which was overwhelmed and collapsed. He said that they had heard all the particulars of what happened from the press, how Dolgarrog was overwhelmed at 9-30 pm on a dark night and that a large part of the population were at a cinema show which saved a lot of lives.

The First Witness

Technical evidence was given by Ralph Freeman of Sir Douglas Fox and Partners. They had designed the dam for Harpur Bros and Co. Consulting Engineers and it was Bott and Stennett who were the contractors who carried out the work.

Mr Freeman maintained that the dam designed by his firm, of which he was a partner, was perfect and that the construction by the contractors Bott and Stennett had been at fault. Mr Freeman pointed out that they were by now no longer in business. To support his submission he produced plans which had been prepared by Mr Hugh Owen, his resident engineer on the phase two construction. This showed a dam wall with 6 ft deep foundations. (One might ask why did he not produce his firms' original plans? The answer to that is that it's most likely they showed the shallower foundations and my guess is they had his name on them!) Mr Freeman was very evasive during questioning as to his involvement. He did not admit that he was the architect, but since he was a partner in the firm he clearly had a major responsibility for the work. It was certain that ACL had a copy as the plans would have been needed for maintenance purposes. Later Jack confirmed this and said:

> had we had reason to suspect the plans of the dam they gave us, we should never have trusted the dam at all.

Mr Freeman described the dam as being a concrete wall: L-shaped of 3,250 ft in length sitting on a subsoil of hard blue clay, boulders and gravel with a layer of peat on top. The burst took place on the long leg of the dam at about

The completed Eigiau Dam

2,156 ft from the beginning of the dam. In describing the breach he offered a photograph showing the hole in the wall to the jury but saying that he did not want to offer it in evidence to the inquest! This meant that the picture would not come into the public domain. A sleight of hand!

When questioned as to whether the dam leaked when completed Mr Freeman said that he had seen the dam shortly after completion, while emphasising that he had no responsibility in connection with it. He said that the concrete was very porous and there were numerous leakages through it. He said that work had been done to check the leaks with considerable success but that it had continued to leak ever since. He went on to assert that he had never seen any evidence of leakage under the dam. He said that leakage through the concrete would have caused him no uneasiness. He had examined the reports of leakage in 1919 but none were at the site of the breach.

The coroner asked Mr Freeman if:

There must have been some latent defect?

Mr Freeman replied:

> I think there was a defect, 'latent' describes it correctly.

The Coroner:

> You had no means of testing for it?

Mr Freeman replied:

> It would have been possible but it was not a procedure that any engineer would expect to undertake.

He saw the dam in 1919 after it had been standing for eight or nine years and came to the conclusion that it was safe. He said that the dam was reliably constructed. Where the burst took place a section 60 ft long by 12 ft deep was carried away under the dam. Since the mishap (its just a mishap now!) he had examined the gap, but he could not say of what the missing part was composed as it had been washed away. What he did find did not correspond with the plan. (The debris of the wall were in place immediately after the burst, we have photographs of it, so by the time of Mr Freeman's visit these must have been removed!).

Mr Freeman went on to say that:

> the concrete structure was of a certain form at one end of the breach and another form at the other end, but he had no way of knowing what was the form between the two.

(The profiles of these ends are substantially different, as can still be seen to-day, in depth, shape and thickness. In fact the thickness of the phase two wall is a foot thinner than that of phase one).

He asserted that the dam wall of phase one was 20 ft 6 ins in depth while the phase two was 26 ft deep. He claimed, and no one challenged it, that on phase one the depth of wall below ground level was only 1 ft 6 ins into the clay while phase two was about 6 ft deep. He went on to claim that his firms plans, (which were not produced), showed that phase one should have had 6 ft deep foundations. The only explanation Mr Freeman could give for the failure was that the last summer was very dry, and the bottom of the wall was uncovered during the dry weather. It was possible that the clay and peat were fissured then, and that allowed the water to flow underneath the foundation. (So blame it on the weather!).

Regarding Coedty Dam he said:

> when Eigiau burst it discharged probably 1 million cubic feet of water onto the lower dam which stood the extraordinary flow in the most wonderful way, and this was the instance of it's great strength. No structure could be built to withstand the quantity of water produced like this was.

Questioned by Mr Proctor (for ACL) about the plans of Eigiau which purported to show the dam being 26 ft in depth Mr Freeman confirmed that the plan was prepared by Mr Owen who was the resident engineer for phase two.

Asked where would Mr Owen could have got the information to prepare the plan Mr Freeman said:

> I cannot tell you.

Also when asked for whom the work on the first section was carried out, his reply was:

> That I cannot tell you – I had no personal association with the construction of the dam.

Asked whether the leakages could have had anything to do with this calamity, his reply was:

> As far as I have information and can judge they had nothing to do with it.

(An Act of God no doubt!).

Mr Stephenson (for the insurers) asked:

> Your firm have in their possession some record of the original sectional drawings that were used in the original construction of the dam?

Mr Freeman answered:

> Yes.

(Why then weren't these plans put before the court rather than the secondhand plans, from a mystery source, prepared by Mr Owen?)

When shown a sectional plan of the dam and asked if it was a drawing of his firm's Mr Freeman said:

> No.

He did admit that his firm had built on top of the 100 ft section of 2 ft deep foundation left by Harpur Bros when they ceased work in 1908. This was a section not signed off and not paid for. When asked did he have any evidence of the thickness and final depth where Harpur Bros finished? Mr Freeman said:

> I cannot answer that question. I was not there and do not know what was done.

Asked if he could not have found out from his records he said:

> We have no records other than this drawing.

Mr Freeman was asked what was the object of recent repair work?

He said:

> The object was to check leakages through the wall at the point that it was carried out.

Asked whether it was definitely a leakage through the dam and not under it at that point, he answered:

> At the point where these repairs were carried out or at any point, I have never seen any evidence of leakage under the dam.

Asked by the coroner of the leakage:

> Would it not be more than you would expect through this concrete?

He replied:

> It is much less in fact; the concrete is very porous and one is naturally surprised to find the leakage is so small.

Evidence from the Watchman at Eigiau

Mr Albert Edward Jones said that he was in his house at the dam on the night. He noticed a flow of water through the dam wall, he claimed, at 9-30 pm. (This is clearly a fiction, as the general agreement from many witnesses is that the explosive collapse of Coedty happened at 9-30 and the torrent reached Dolgarrog five minutes later. Since his house was over half a mile way from the breach of Eigiau and it was a very dark night there is no possibility that he would have been able to see anything, he must have heard Coedty collapsing). He rang the Works only to be told to hang on for a minute as the supervisor was taking another call. He claimed he had an electric shock from the phone and realising he had been cut off, he rang the watchman at Cowlyd and asked him to alert the works.

The Coroner said that even two minutes in such a case might have made all the difference. (At the very least had the power house staff been warned, they could have helped to relieve the pressure by opening the drain valves of the Coedty pipe. It was widely known among the workers that this had not been done).

The Sluicegate Operator's house at Eigiau

W. J. Roberts

A Mr W.J. Roberts, one of the partners in a group who originally owned the water rights in the area, before they were taken over by the ACL said that he had observed leakages in 1923. When questioned whether he had reported them, he said:

> I only noticed them as I was passing.

Then asked did he never think of mentioning them he replied:

> everyone knew about them.

Crossley Colley

Crossley Colley, the Construction Manager for ACL gave evidence that the dam was 4,600 ft in length, with 1,300 ft of that a peat bank at the end of the north section. He clarified who had been responsible for the construction. He said that Sir Douglas Fox and Partners had designed the dam and in the first phase the engineers in charge of the work were Harpur Bros.

For the second phase Sir Douglas Fox and Partners were in charge of that work. Bott and Stennett were the contractors in both cases.

He described how inspections of all the hydraulic works were undertaken once a week by the water supervisor. He said that they had a man resident at the lake who was a sluice gate keeper. His duties were to regulate the water as instructed by the power house.

He stated that minor repairs and patching had been carried out on the dam from 1921. Mr Colley went on to say that there was not, during all of these operations or since, the slightest evidence of any water coming underneath the dam. He repeated that nowhere did the water leak except through the concrete which he would describe as porous, more porous than would be expected in ordinary concrete construction. He said that the dam had a capacity of 160 million cubic foot. Regarding the phone system from the lakes the lines converged near the power house and the flood swept away the telephone poles which caused the failure of the phones.

Asked about a report that there had been an overflow from the leat just a week or ten days before the disaster. He replied that:

> It was only a normal overflow.

(Enough to cause flooding across the road in Porth Llwyd and serious concern to the residents!).

Evidence from P.C. Jones, Tal-y-bont

PC Jones of Tal-y-bont, who had been a stonemason before joining the police force, said that when he visited the site of the breach on 5 November he estimated that there was a gap under the dam wall 72 ft long by 15 ft in depth. He went on to describe the construction of the dam wall. He said that the concrete did not appear to have been mixed properly, there were many lumps of dry material and boulders mixed in and also there appeared to be no foundation to the dam. He also mentioned that during the two preceding summers of 1924 and 25 the nearby Parish Road had been ankle deep in water opposite the gap and the place was a swamp.

He went on to say that:

> you could see the blue clay and judging by the elevation of the mountains they need not have gone far to get rock for a foundation.

One might mention, but it was not pointed out at the inquest, that there had been a drought during both these periods and that the water in the dam would not have reached the dam wall. This policeman was, in effect, the only independent witness to give evidence as to the construction of the dam. He could not by any means have been described as an expert witness. Here was a stone mason giving opinions about a civil engineering construction. His declaration that there were no foundations to the dam wall showed that he misunderstood the construction of this type of dam which does not require foundations going down to bedrock.

The dam is technically a mass concrete gravity dam. This is because it is a wall which is narrower at the top becoming wider at its base and relies on its weight for its stability. It does not necessarily have to have deep foundations and was constructed of concrete and aggregate. This was the norm when Eigiau was built. Nowadays this would have to be reinforced concrete.

Expert not called

An anonymous expert who inspected the breach shortly after the event, but who was not called at the inquest, told the *Llandudno Advertiser* that the hole in the dam was 30 ft wide. He stated that it was quite safe to walk along the dam wall over the breach on what in effect was a bridge. If the policeman's estimate of the height of the gap, 15 ft, was measured from the bottom of the dam foundation, then since the height of the dam is in fact 26.5 ft, there would have been 11.5 ft of wall remaining above the breach. This is just a hole blown in the wall, bearing no relationship to the wide gap shown in later photographs. These photographs were taken after the wall had been dynamited by ACL to make the breach much wider to mislead investigators into concluding that this was the cause of the disaster.

Harpur Brothers

Mr Alan Randolph Harpur, of Harpur Brothers and Company Engineers, stated that it was his company, under whose supervision the first section of the dam was constructed to a design by Ralph Freeman. He produced a sheet prepared by their resident engineer at the time, which purported to show that the work was surveyed and certified to a point indicated on Oct. 9 1908. After that date work was continued for another 100 ft approximately of a 2 ft deep foundation, but that part was never certified and for this his firm was not responsible. The work was afterwards completed by other engineers of the Aluminium Corporation. It was at that point that the break took place. Replying to a Mr Proctor representing the Power Company, Mr Harpur said he had no personal knowledge of what he had stated (as he was only seven years old in 1907) except from correspondence in the office. (That makes him a very credible witness!).

The plan he had put in agreed with Mr Freemans's plan showing a dam wall depth of 26 ft at the spot where the break occurred. Mr Harpur had not been to the spot since the accident and he was not prepared to dispute Mr Freeman's measurements showing that the depth of the wall at the south end of the break was only 20 ft 6 ins, instead of the 26 ft shown on the plan. It was the duty of Harpur's clerk of the works to see that the cement was properly mixed and if it was not properly mixed it was his firm's servant's fault. He admitted that the foundations were not to the proper level and that the whole of the break was within the uncertified scope of their work.

Answering the foreman of the jury, Mr Harpur said that the depth of the concrete at the north end was 26 ft but at the south end it was only 20 ft 6 ins.

Lionel Taylor

Mr Lionel Taylor said he was clerk of the works and resident engineer partly in the service of Messrs Harpur Bros as well as the original Aluminium Corporation. He had among his assistants an admirable man named Wilson, now dead, whose duty it was to see that concrete was properly mixed and the foundations were carried out to the correct depth. He pointed out that on the day that they stopped work, as he had indicated on their plan, the original quantity of concrete provided for was 17,200 cubic yards and they had already used up 16,000 cubic yards of this with still a substantial part of the dam yet to be built This was put down to the fact that, in places, they had go down deeper than the plans indicated because of variations in the terrain.

Answering Mr Proctor (for ACL), Mr Taylor said that it was Wilson's duty to see that the work was properly carried out. Mr Taylor admitted that Wilson was not competent to measure and layout the work but Messrs Harpur had left him there in charge of that work. Mr Taylor could only explain the differences in the planned and actual depth of the concrete at this point by supposing that Wilson had not carried out his work according to instructions.

James Loftus Owen

Mr James Loftus Owen, Birmingham, supervising engineer for Messrs Harpur Brothers as assistant to Mr Taylor, agreed that at the point where the break occurred, the evidence bore out the suggestion that the concrete was not carried out to the proper depth. He considered Mr Taylor, as Messrs Harpur's employee, responsible for that. Mr Owen became responsible for the phase two part of the scheme by Freeman, Fox and partners and he carried it out according to the plan. (Including of course the rubbish concrete construction!)

Edward Humphreys

Mr Edward Humphreys, water superintendent for ACL, said his duty was to report as to water storage. He had reported leakages, but could not say that the spot where the break occurred showed any leakage. He said that depending on the level of water in the dam you could see water spouting out through the concrete just below ground level. He was sure that the water was coming through the concrete and not from under the dam.

The Coroner Sums Up

Addressing the jury, the coroner told them that several witnesses who were in Dolgarrog on the night were present now, but they could only describe what happened after the burst, and that the cause of the mischief was really the bursting of the dam. He went on:

> You can imagine what happened on that night and you have seen a lot in the press about it. Do you want to hear anything about it?

The Jury foreman said:

> No, we know all about that.

The coroner then summed up observing that the persons responsible for the work, where the breach occurred, were the contractors Bott and Stennett. The resident engineer Mr Hugh Owen, employed by Freeman Fox and Partners, should also have made sure that it was properly carried out. The person responsible for actually mixing the concrete could not be traced. (How convenient!). He noted that the Eigiau Dam had stood for fifteen years but a time came when it could stand no longer, hence the breach. The water flowed down to the Coedty Dam which could not possibly

to hang on as the line was engaged. A couple of minutes later the line went dead.

Mr Arthur R. Hughes reporter for the *Llandudno Advertiser* who was the father of the deceased, Mrs Taylor, was allowed to ask questions of Mr Crossley Colley. He asked:

> had the watchman stated times to visit the dam?

Mr Colley replied that:

> it was dark and stormy.

At this the coroner chimed in:

> The water would be flowing pretty near half an hour, and must have been doing so before the man at the dam noticed it

Mr Hughes persisted:

> What period of time did he patrol the dam?

Mr Colley replied:

> The principal duty of Albert Edward Jones was to work the sluices. As more machines went on at the works he had to give them more water.

Mr Hughes:

> Would it not have been better to patrol the dam periodically?

The coroner, eager to put an end to this potentially awkward line of questioning said that:

> the accident was caused by the unexpected giving way of the dam wall and no doubt Jones would have been indoors at the time.

Chapter 10

Independent Reports

The Gibbs Report

Sir Alexander Gibbs and Partners, were asked by ACL to make a report that was intended to indicate the best method of repairing the damage at Eigiau and Coedty as well as to keep the Home Office happy. Completed in June 1926 it was very revealing of information lost since 1911.Numerous trial pits were dug up to 20 ft in depth below the surface as well as a borehole 40 ft deep near the breach.

They concluded:

> the depth to which the foundation is carried into good ground... particularly in the long arm... falls short of what is required to make a satisfactory and safe construction to hold water.

It was not possible to determine whether the blow-out was due to a critically enlarged void in the concrete or a seepage path in the glacial clay strata under the wall. It was also generally agreed that at the point of failure there had been a seepage for several years hence the flooded road nearby. They found that the concrete was in places very bad and generally poor. There was evidence of bad workmanship and that water had infiltrated through it for a considerable period. The honeycombed nature of the concrete at the breach showed evidence of deposits of peat, left by peat laden water which had accumulated in the voids left during construction. These spaces were up to 3 ins in diameter under the stone displacers. These deficiencies can still be seen to-day on the phase two end wall.

Their remit, of course, was not to apportion blame for the failure but one can only conclude that the leakage problems were endemic from the start and that no serious remedial action had been taken apart from some desultory patching up. The maintenance gangs had much more important things to do across the valley. One might also conclude that Gibbs and Partners, who were leading lights in the Civil Engineering milieu, would not want to rock the boat for other professionals in the industry. Scratch my back and I will scratch yours – otherwise known as the Masonic handshake!

The Royal Geographical Society Study

Their 1928 report entitled *A Topographical Study of the Flood-Swept Course of the Porth Llwyd Above Dolgarrog* by two eminent professors who looked at the bursting of dams above Dolgarrog as an opportunity for securing a complete record of the notable changes of topography, which had been produced by the flow of a determinate amount of water along a British river's course, and to obtain photographic records of the geological effects of the debacle.

Most interesting is the personal thanks, on the first page of the document, they give to Freeman Fox and Partners and Mr Ralph Freeman in particular who gave them authoritative information regarding the general plan of concentration and storage of the run-off from the hills. This enabled the investigators to estimate the rate at which the waters were released. They go on:

> it is only right to say that neither Mr Freeman, nor any member of his firm, was responsible for the original

> construction of the dam beneath which the flood waters escaped from Llyn Eigiau!

Why approach Ralph Freeman if he had never been involved in the project to build the dams?

As to the sequence of events that led to the blow out (this is the technically correct way to describe what happened) one has to sift the evidence. In 1928 The Royal Geographical Society, being independent and quite close to the event, were able to point to many tell tale features still remaining to give clues to what happened on the night.

We know from evidence at the inquest that there had been water escaping through the dam since before it was completed and it was endemic to the structure. Flooding of the road nearby during the two preceding years, which was stated at the inquest, may well have been a red herring. To-day, in the summer, the same road has pools on it up to ankle depth – this despite the fact that the dam is in effect now empty. It appears that this water is just natural run off from the peat layers in the valley.

The night watchman claims that he first became aware of the problems at 9 pm. In the total darkness of a stormy November night he would not have been able to see anything wrong unless he was actually walking the wall, when in fact he admitted in evidence that he was in his house at the time. Also the Coedty Dam which was overtopping was 2 miles away from his house. The event would most likely have started as the increase in a leak through the wall, which was gradually enlarged in size by the erosion of the water flow. This is where the faulty concrete becomes crucial, Also this was where the phase one and two walls were joined. The valley below the dam is very wide and the distance to the Coedty Dam about two miles. This allowed the escaping water to spread itself widely – so that it was not a raging torrent concentrated on a narrow channel. The level of water in the Eigiau Dam was variously estimated by RGS based on information supplied by Ralph Freeman, as up to 20 ft at the breach. This is clearly an exaggeration as measurements to-day show that the dam wall is only 16.5 ft above ground level. The level of the water could only have been, at most, 11 ft, so the actual pressure of the water flowing, was nearly half of what the estimates suggested.

Another clue as to the way the blow out developed can be seen to-day. To quote from the Royal Geographical Society investigation:

> The momentum of a torrent at every point tends to carry it straight on. Yet the track of the water where it leaves the breach immediately meanders – it has an S bend rather than carrying straight on as would be expected. This might indicate that the flow was substantial, but not a torrent. The head of water at the breach, of a maximum of 12 ft, would not have created as great a torrent as was claimed at the inquest.

The dam breach showing the run off from the blow-out

The RGS found, by studying the geology of the valley and gorge that the massive boulders, remnants of the last Ice Age, had been dislodged and propelled by the torrent from within the gorge between Coedty and the village – not from within the valley above.

London University Report

A report on an investigation by the Department of Civil Engineering of the City University of London in 1973 is very revealing. They were studying Eigiau as an example of how not to build a gravity dam. They carried out a detailed survey and in their findings agreed with what Mr Freeman had said. They showed scale plans of the dam walls each side of the breach which they published in their University magazine: Quest. The profile and design of the dam at each end of the breach are significantly different. The right hand side wall – phase two, was made up of the much criticised faulty concrete work but with foundations over 6 ft deep; whilst on the left hand side – phase one, appears to be of perfectly well constructed concrete but with only 2 ft 6 ins of foundation. Also the thickness of the right hand wall is about one foot thinner than the left one. Are we to believe that the negligent constructors suddenly had a eureka moment and put in these extra foundations and changed the design without the Supervisory Engineer noticing, and at variance with the plans by Ralph Freeman? Very unlikely! It would have required a completely new design of shuttering for the concrete to do this.

Chapter 11

The real cause of the disaster

Commentary on the Findings of the Inquests and Investigations

We have four sources of information – the newspaper reports of the time, the documents of the ACL, the inquest reports and the follow up investigations by independent bodies. In fact plans of the construction of the Eigiau Dam, which were put before the inquest have apparently gone missing. The first inquest was the crucial one – this was the forum for exposing who was responsible for the disaster. In those days there was no provision for a public inquiry into a dam disaster, so the inquest was the only way of finding out what had happened and deciding who might be responsible.

The question must be asked how it was that the coroner expounded to the court and jury his belief concerning what had gone on, even before he had heard any of the evidence! It looks as if there had been some pre-inquest briefing going on!

The inquests show that there was only one conclusion to be made – it was a game of pass the buck, with very high stakes!

All the principle participants were negligent at one stage or another – there is little doubt that they got together with the aim of confusing what they perceived as a compliant coroner. They were fortunate that there were no serious legal challenges. The only legal representatives were there for the North.Wales Power Company, the insurance companies, the County Council and the Government Electricity Commission.

ACL needed a result which put the blame on a fall guy – preferably someone way down the pecking order, and that is the result they got in spades! The Resident Clerk of the Works – the 'admirable' but now deceased Mr Wilson, and the person actually responsible for mixing the concrete who could not be traced, were perfect scapegoats!

Had it been shown that ACL had been negligent in the maintenance of Eigiau the insurance companies might have decided not to pay out and this could have been the end of ACL.

Issues addressed

The four issues addressed were: was the dam constructed according to the plans, were those plans defective, who was responsible for the alleged faulty concrete work and was the maintenance adequate?

The coroner appeared to be floundering when faced by the expert witnesses all of whom had something hide. Ralph Freeman claimed that the construction had not followed the plans for the dam which his company had prepared, in particular in relation to the depth of the foundations. Mr James Loftus Owen was the Resident Engineer on phase one of the construction. Mr Owen agreed that at the point where the break occured the evidence showed that the concrete was not carried out to the specified depth of 6 ft – but only 2 ft 6 ins and he considered Mr Taylor, as an employee of Harpur Bros., responsible for that. He (the witness) only became responsible for the construction of phase two of the plan by Freeman, Fox and Partners. But the deviation from Freeman's plans regarding the depth of the foundations, could not have been done without Mr Owen's explicit instructions. In fact the misleading plans put before the coroner were drawn by him and accepted as a record by the coroner. He was also in charge on the second phase of work in 1910-1911. This may have implied that the plans as shown indicated a foundation depth of 6 ft. These plans are quite clearly not the original ones that Freeman drew for phase one of the dam so why were those not produced? With sleight of hand Freeman deliberately misled the inquiry by pretending that his plans for the whole project were the same as these.

The clue is that Ralph Freeman admitted, almost as an aside in his evidence, that the profile of the dam walls at each side of the breach were different but he had no means of knowing what was the shape of the wall between the two, as the base had fallen. It was being claimed that the blow out had occurred in the termination of the first section which Mr Harpur stated, had not been signed off by his firm nor had been paid for.

He produced a photograph of the blow out in the dam wall to the inquest. The jury saw this photograph but Mr Freeman insisted that this picture should not be part of the evidence! One might ask why?

Concerning the dam construction – let us look at the suggestion that the blow out began by water escaping under the dam wall. At the present time the phase one wall is 16.5 ft above ground level. In the evidence from Mr Freeman at the inquest, he stated that this wall was actually a total of 20.5 ft in height. A sectional plan from the time shows this. This actually equates with the foundation being 4 ft into the blue clay not the 2 ft 6 ins he claimed. It was stated that the wall was embedded at varying depths. Clay is an excellent material for containing water. Farmers in the past, constructed dew ponds using clay. In the case of Eigiau the weight of the wall on the clay would have made a very effective seal. It is unlikely that clay would have dried and cracked as was suggested, because evidence was given of ground water in the vicinity of the dam even during two

A piece of railway line embedded in the dam wall

previous drought years. The peat beds in that location were estimated to be 4-6 ft in depth. In fact the ground around the area of the burst is still very boggy even to this day. The Royal Geographical Survey tells us that the phase two wall was set from 1-2 ft into the clay. I would suggest that they could not have known this, as by this time the exposed foundations had been expertly covered up with a neat skirt of stone work. Taking the actual

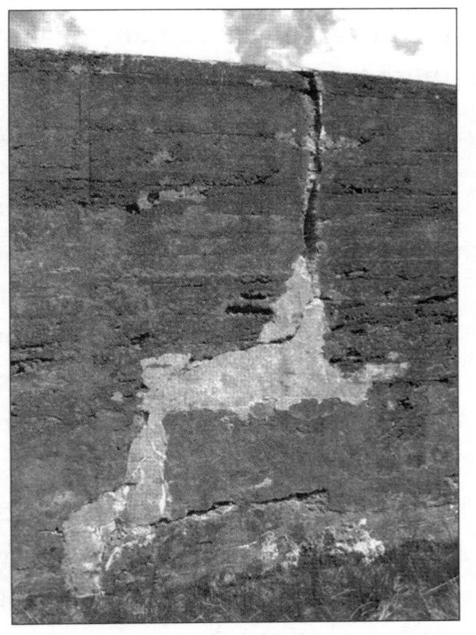

An example of the patching and the cracks in the Eigiau Dam wall

foundations as being 6 ft deep then this would be more than adequate to ensure a good watertight seal.

This points to the actual concrete work being faulty and therefore being exposed by the breach. The end of the wall of phase two is one foot thinner than phase one, and with rubbish concrete full of rubble, stone spacers and even bits of railway line – in other words a cowboy job, even though it did have the significantly deeper foundations. To-day one can see that the dam walls are riddled with cracks, some which had been patched up – a sieve would be an apt description. Freeman, Fox and Partners must ultimately take responsibility for this work as the engineers in charge.

The Fictional Night Watchman

His evidence differs from the dramatic story which was told to the press at the time, that he tried to make the call but got an electric shock from the phone and then made his way on foot over the mountain to Cowlyd, to get the watchman there to raise the alarm. As there were no overhead electric cables running through the Eigiau Valley, this makes the shock story unlikely. In fact the only such power cables were routed through the Cowlyd Valley – well away from the floods. Apart from that, telephones even in that era, were unable to give an electric shock to the user. If he only became aware of the burst at 9 pm he must have been asleep, as by this time there was serious flooding in Dolgarrog.

So there we have it! Mr Jones, the watchman, was not required to patrol the dams – only to control the water flowing from them, when directed by the powerhouse. He was in his house at Eigiau just two miles from Coedty when that dam collapsed, at about 9-30 pm with a thunderous roar and explosions heard several miles away at Llanrwst and Tal-y-bont. The claim originally made was that he became aware of the burst at 8-45 pm then tried to warn Dolgarrog at 9 pm. I suggest that this story was planted by someone in authority from ACL – there is no evidence that Mr Jones was actually interviewed by a journalist. In those days the word of an official was not often questioned and anyway it was probably a case of:

> don't let the facts get in the way of a good story.

But ACL needed the story as they were then able to claim that he had tried to give the alarm, but had failed because of circumstances outside his control – he bravely did his duty!

No Water Management Strategy

It is quite clear that ACL did not have any strategy for managing water flows through their leats, pipes and tunnels and into their dams and this was a very significant matter. One can guess that ACL had been pre-occupied over the years with water shortages, and the concept of an excess of water was quite alien to the management. The watchman was in reality just a sluice gate operator – he had no other responsibility. ACL had had two warnings: in 1924 when the Cowlyd Dam came perilously close to collapse; and then just eleven days before the disaster when there was bad flooding in Dolgarrog – which was described by ACL as just the normal overflow of a leat. They played it down, but it was more important than they suggested. The nature and design of a leat is to deposit water into a dam. By definition this requires it should empty into the dam at the maximum water level.

If in fact a leat had overflowed, unless of course there was a design fault, then the dam must have been overflowing eleven days before the disaster. As to the seriousness of this overflow we can only speculate. If nothing else, it showed that there was too much water coming into the dam and the spillway could not cope with the overflow.

If Eigiau had been properly monitored that night, the excessive flow over the spillway could have been reduced by closing the sluice gates which fed water into the dam through the tunnel from Afon Dulyn. As for the water flowing into Coedty through the low level leats from both Afon Ddu and Afon Dulyn, they could also have been stopped off. In addition, had the power house been warned, they would have been able to stop generating and use a drain in the pipeline from Coedty to further reduce the pressure.

The breach in the Eigiau Dam was almost a sideshow contributing just a trickle compared to the other inflows into Coedty. But it got ACL off the hook and it suited them to blame the disaster on just this one cause.

The Spillways

The Royal Geographical Society study suggested that the level of water in Eigiau as a result of the storm, could have been up to 2 ft above the spillway (the overflow) which was 35 ft wide. The spillway at Coedty which was 25 ft wide according to plans of the time would not have been able to

Eigiau Dam showing spillway and sluice

cope with that amount of water from the Eigiau overflow. The water being discharged into the Afon Porthllwyd would have been considerable. The extra water now coming down from the blow out would only have added a minor amount to this torrent.

Quite clearly the failure of Coedty was caused by the design faults of Ralph Freeman. He did not provide an adequate width of spillway.

When Coedty was rebuilt, after hydrological tests were carried out with models, he increased the spillway to 58 ft. In 1956 the spillway was widened again by the Central Electricity Authority which at that time was the owmer of the dam. Add the water flow from the Eigau spillway to the increasing flow from the dam wall blow out and the leats, and you have a receipe for disaster.

Haste

It is fairly clear that there was undue haste to get the inquest over and done with – in fact. it took just a month. There would have been no time to get a proper independent investigation as we would expect to-day. The Gibbs report, which had been ordered by the Home Office was not available til June the following year.

A Cover Up

It was a disaster just waiting to happen. Once the initial clearing up had been done the ACL management realised that they had no reliable excuses to explain the events, so they urgently engineered a cover up. The modest blow out through the Eigiau Dam wall was the first step. The dynamited section where the blow out had been became a 150 ft wide gap, littered with broken concrete They quite rapidly removed most of this material – many tons of it, before the Stuctural Engineers from Gibbs were able to get to the site. Gibbs reported that they were unable to deduce the construction of the dam at the breach as all the remains had been swept away in the torrent. Then ACL claimed that the much newer Coedty Dam could not have stood up to the the flood waters that ensued – it was just an act of God! There were some tricky questions asked at the inquest about the actual materials and construction of the Eigiau Dam wall – mainly who was to blame for the criminally dangerous design and the shoddy work involved? No questions were asked about the design and construction of Coedty. A suitably briefed coroner was all that they needed and got!

Today you can see the site as it was left, with a big empty depression between the two dam wall ends. But somebody must have thought it looked a bit untidy – so after removing the debris they built a stone skirt round to the base of the phase two, right hand exposed dam wall end! It serves no obvious purpose but it looks neat and tidy! But why should anyone bother to do that? I would suggest it was built to

The elaborate cover up, the wall around the base of the Eigiau Dam wall

hide the fact that the wall was substantially different from its opposite a few yards away. It looks much like someone had tidied up a crime scene! But there is one item of evidence they left behind – the remains of a typical quarry truck, now on its side and very rusty, which they may have been used to carry the incriminating evidence away from the site.

The evidence also suggested that it was most likely that the blow out occurred at the actual junction of the phase one wall and the later completed phase two. It would have been difficult to make a satisfactory union between the two walls, particularly as they were of a different shape and thickness – thus presenting a potential weakness. This is most likely as the 6 ft deep foundations of phase two are unlikely to have been undermined. The evidence of this would have been exposed in the debris hence the need to get rid of them.

Put simply, the dam was designed by Ralph Freeman of Freeman, Fox and Partners, who employed Harpur Bros to supervise the construction, which was carried out by Bott and Stennett. Harpurs employed a resident Clerk of Works, a Mr Wilson who lived on site. A Mr Lionel Taylor was employed both by ACL to whom he was the Clerk of Works and Harpur Bros to whom he was the Resident Engineer. A Mr James Loftus Owen was also a Resident Engineer who had made the original survey for ACL and was in the pay of Harpur Bros. For phase two a Mr Hugh Owen was the Resident Engineer reporting to Freeman. I hope that is all clear! With all this supervision it would have been foolhardy – if not impossible for Bott and Stennett to deviate from Freeman's plans and to use poor construction methods and shallow foundations.

Apportioning Blame

The real cause of the disaster, only mentioned almost in

passing at the inquest, was the overtopping of the Coedty Dam which is two miles downstream from Eigiau. The quantity of water flowing into this dam was too much for the design of the spillway and consequently the water overtopped the dam wall. This might not have been important had the water not eroded away the exposed soil on the downstream side of the dam, leading to the whole dam collapsing in one great explosive eruption. Coedty was designed as essentially an earth bank with a thin concrete membrane running through it to stop seepage and the dam inner side wall was covered with stones cemented in place to stop wave erosion. The downside earth wall had no such protection – which is quite normal construction for a soil dam.

A Near Catastrophe at Cowlyd

This was also the design of the recently constructed Cowlyd Dam. One year earlier in 1924, strong winds sent waves crashing over the dam wall. There was an immediate threat of a major collapse because of the soil erosion on the downside of the dam. Had this happened then a huge quantity of water would have been released – a thousand times greater than that which hit Dolgarrog. It is said that even Llanrwst would have been flooded. In the event, frantic efforts by workmen with sandbags saved the day.

Subsequently the wave wall at Cowlyd was increased in height along with a layer of concrete applied covering the soil on the downside.

Looking at the Eigiau Dam forensically there are a number of features that give the game away. There is a tide mark on the Eigiau Dam wall, at the breach, which shows that the depth of water at that point would have normally been about 4 ft for much of the year. We know the wall had been leaking like a sieve, despite patching since it was built

The Cowlyd Dam wall, showing the re-inforcements to the downside which prevents errosion by overtopping

and what was described as a blow out at the inquest had, in reality, been just somewhat larger than usually expected, so it was not considered by ACL management to need immediate attention. After all, to deal with it, the water level would need to be dropped by draining the resevoir and that might upset production in the factory. Come the first serious rains of autumn, estimated to have increased the level at the time of the disaster to 12 ft, the pressure would have substantially increased the water flow eroding and widening the hole. What the witnesses saw, many hours later after the flood had receded, was a now much bigger hole.

The flooding in Dolgarrog some 11 days before the disaster was a precursor for the main event. No one had been warned. The reason, given by an official of ACL, that it was just an overflow of the leats at Coedty, nothing to worry about! Looking closely at these leats now reveals that it was not possible that they could have overtopped. What had happened was that the water had flooded over the dam wall and in doing so partly eroded the downside which was just soil with a turf topping. The dam could have been dangerously weakened.

This, you might have thought, would have been the time to arrange for a watchman to supervise and an emergency alarm scheme to warn the people of the village of the dangers of a flood, along with repairs to the dam wall to make it safe. It appears nothing was done. The workforce, which was at that time building a grand drive up to Plas Jack, could have been diverted to this more pressing problem. But no, Harry Jack's mansion was more important! After the disaster work stopped at Plas Jack and the part finished drive can still be seen to this day!

Coedty was reconstructed after the disaster but still had problems with leaks in the core wall. In 1956, the then owners the Central Electricity Authority, carried out improvements to the catchment area of the dam with extended leats. In this connection it became apparent that the 1926 spillway was still inadequate and so it was rebuilt – ironically to a design by Freeman, Fox and Partners! The leaks continued until major reconstruction works on the dam were undertaken in 1972.

In Conclusion

I have long been fascinated by the causes of accidents and disasters. I spent a large part of my career, over forty years, covering such events as a news cameraman for BBC Wales. It is well accepted, that apart from unpredictable natural disasters, there is almost always a thread of human failure leading inexorably, step by banal step, to an unhappy end.

The root causes are usually financial or political – or more likely a lack of will on behalf of politicians, often a mixture of both!

Taking the case of Eigiau, the design was to say the least, inadequate and the construction was criminally bad. Had there been legislation regarding the safety of such structures at that time, then there can be no doubt that ACL. would never have been allowed to fill it with water. There was then no legislation controlling the construction and inspection of reservoirs – despite a the serious collapse of the Bradfield Dam in Yorkshire in 1864 when 245 people lost their lives. Soon afterwards a Select Committee on the Waterworks Bill made a number of recommendations regarding safety, but the fall of the Liberal Government meant that the bill was forgotten. That is, until Dolgarrog when the then Home Secretary sprang into life to demand an independent examination of all dams. This eventually led to the introduction of the Resevoir (Safety Provisions) Act 1930, which required that every ten years an engineer with expertise in dam design should inspect any dam containing more than half a million gallons of water. The fatal flaw in the Act was that Local Authorities were not obliged to draw up lists of reservoirs in their areas. Repairs and inspections were often not carried out. In 1975 the government passed the Resevoirs Act compelling County Councils to draw up a list of all resevoirs in their County and ensure that they were properly inspected. The Act was implemented in four stages, so that it was not fully in effect until 1987. At one point, the then Thatcher Government was proposing to ignore it altogether. In 1981 Giles Shaw for the Department of the Environment stated he was quite sure that problems with resevoir safety could be met by the 1930 Act!

Serious Leaks

It was quite clear from the start that Eigiau leaked like a sieve. Yet only the most feeble efforts were made to stop the seepage. A large amount of ACL.'s manpower and materials had been diverted to the grand Plas Maenan project. It is quite clear that the Directors of ACL were aware of the shortcomings of the dam from the earliest days and that could be the reason that in 1923 they authorised the construction of a tunnel to take water from Eigiau to Cowlyd but it was not completed until 1928. This would have reduced Eigiau to what it is to-day, a natural Ice Age lake.

The next failure and the most serious was the design of the new Coedty Dam. The spillway was quite inadequate being only 25 ft wide while Eigiau's spillway was 36 ft wide. Apart from the water coming in from the overspill at Eigiau and down the Afon Porthllwyd to Coedty, there were the two low level leats that fed directly into Coedty from Afon Dulyn and Afon Ddu. The internal side of the dam was coated in rock and concrete but fatally, the downside of this soil dam was not protected from being washed away by an overspill, as we have heard had nearly happened the year before at the Cowlyd Dam.

Clearly the warning was ignored as just eleven days before the disaster, Dolgarrog was seriously flooded following heavy rainfall. This could only have been the result of water spilling over the dam wall which would have partly eroded the downside of the dam.

I know that in soil dam construction it would not normally be the practice to protect the downside from erosion. However, with the now weakened dam, exceptional measures were needed – particularly supervison when there was high rainfall.Also the time to set up a flood warning system. None of these matters were brought up at the inquest!

It reminds me of maths at school where we had to calculate how long a bath would take to fill with x gallons per minute coming in and y gallons per minute going out through the overflow. I suppose we could then work out how long it would be before the bathroom would be flooded – very useful!

Then we have the night-watchman who was not required to watch the dams at night! He was later described as the valve keeper. According to the coroner he was in his house beside Eigiau when the dams broke. He then lied about the time of his warning which was made after Coedty had collapsed. This was added to by the modest blow out through the hole in the wall of Eigiau. This was almost certainly caused by the appalling construction of the dam. It appears that this leak had probably been running for quite some time, maybe days – starting as a modest trickle but increasing as the wall disintegrated. The size of the gap in the wall as seen in photographs of the time is misleading. What they show is the result of the work of ACL. who used dynamite to remove the bridge over the breech – giving the impression that it was a major collapse rather than a minor burst.

So now to the villains: Ralph Freeman, a junior with Sir Douglas Fox and Partners. Maybe Sir Douglas gave the job of designing the Eigiau Dam to his understrapper as something not too ambitious for him to cut his teeth on. It appears he was out of his depth from the start both with the design and supervision of the construction of both phase one and phase two. He made another fatal mistake in 1924 when he designed the Coedty Dam.

One would hope he had learned some lessons. The newly knighted Sir Ralph Freeman went on to design the Sydney Harbour Bridge. This would have been crucial to his career and had he been shown to have been negligent with regard to Eigiau and Coedty then his professional standing would have been seriously dented. For him the stakes were high – but with the help of 'Y Pobl Fawr' he got away with it!

Then there is Harry Jack who was the captain of the ship. He could not have claimed ignorance because he was implicated from the start with the failings of Eigiau and noticably was not called to give evidence at the inquest. The Plas Maenan improvements were much more important to him than the safety of the people of Dolgarrog!

Now who was to be blamed? The inquest put it all on the estimable Mr Wilson who oversaw the mixing of the concrete but he was now deceased and the man actually doing the work could not be traced! That was the result that 'Y Bobl Fawr' needed.

However, the question of the night watchman and the timing of the warning to the works did come under scrutiny – not at the first and main inquest, but at the third – into the death of Mrs Dorothy Taylor. Here at last questions were asked about the actual **timings** of the call from Llyn Eigiau. Too late, by now the foxes had sprung the coup and were well away. Sighs of relief all round in the directors boardroom! No-one else was interested in those days before the advent of public inquiries.

Chapter 12

The clear up

The Aftermath

The disaster – while it was a major blow to the people of Dolgarrog, the loss of the two dams was very serious for ACL – more so for the work force who became unemployed, though many had temporary work doing the clearing up.

In May 1926 Jack reported to the Board that he has arranged for a hut from the Cowlyd site to be re-erected in the village for use as the school and as the church had been destroyed – only the cross and the bell survived intact, services were to be held in the Assembly Hall. Then the Board authorised the conversion of the Working Men's Institute (originally Tyddyn Farm) into a church and house for the curate. The barn – which had been used as the billiard room became the nave as it was the only part of the building which had an east-west axis. It was operational from June. Only a small proportion of the population of Dolgarrog were regular church goers. In the 1930's with an electoral roll of 119 only twenty at most of the faithful would attend Sunday services The general population of Dyffryn Conwy who were devout followers of the Biblical requirements of The Lord's Day, regarded the people of Dolgarrog as a Godless lot. The factory had to be kept running seven days a week with both day and night shifts, because the furnaces could not be allowed to go out. However the workers did not work on Sunday afternoons, presumably so that they could enjoy a bit of peace and privacy with their wives while the children were at the Sunday School – which was well attended!

It is somewhat hazy as to whether those who lost their homes and loved ones were properly compensated. Many were probably grateful to still have a job when the factory re-opened. Fortunately many of the Abden Clee houses were empty and available to re-house those who were homeless. The pressure was on and the house building scheme was completed in 1926.

Education

After the disaster, the school was held in Bankfield House but with the growing numbers of pupils they also had to hold classes in the Sillans and the Aviary.

In 1927 with the problem of overcrowding getting worse ACL gifted a plot of land to the county for the building of a Central School on the road to Tal-y-bont. This was completed in 1937 catering for children up to the age of fourteen. There was also an infants section. Welsh was taught as a second language.

Norwegian Adventure

While the Carneddau had seemed to be ideal for electricity generation due to its high rainfall, this turned out to be too seasonal for all the year round production. ACL looked to other parts of the world for its reduction process, where water supplies were more abundant and reliable. In 1907 the British Aluminium Corporation of Scotland had acquired a hydro reduction plant at Stangfjord on the west coast of Norway. In 1926 Harry Jack and two fellow directors paid a visit there, and it was agreed that ACL should also establish a Norwegian reduction works to supplement Dolgarrog. Fortunately between 1914 and 1923 the Norwegian Government had invested nearly £2 million on a factory for the smelting of Zinc concentrates. This had been abandoned when they found that regulations during and after the war made it impossible to get raw materials from Australia, which was at that time the main source of supply.

Situated on a fjord washed by the Gulfstream and therefore free from ice all year round, made the shipping of raw materials and the smelted aluminium assured. There was an immediate, substantial supply of hydro electricity with options for more. This meant that the factory would be able to produce 22,000 tons a year, compared with Dolgarrog which could only manage a tenth of that at best. ACL took out a lease on the factory and formed A/S Haugvik Smelteverke to operate the Norwegian plant. The Bauxite refining works at Hebburn on Tyne was now reconstituted as the International Aluminium Company to supply Bauxite to both north Wales and Norway. Jack was the Managing Director and other directors were A/S HS board members. A team of skilled personnel was sent from Dolgarrog to Norway to teach the techniques of smelting to the local workers.

The first ingots were received at Dolgarrog in January 1927 but were of substandard quality and it was some time before this was remedied. Then there was the problem of import duty! Although the Norwegian Company was a subsidiary of ACL it was still required that duty should be paid. This was not the case if the imports were from a Commonwealth country, so it was more profitable to divert the Haugvik metal to another country via Antwerp in exchange for an equal tonnage to be delivered to north Wales from Canada.

Jacks Last Stand

It must be said that at a time when north Wales still had its wealth tied up in landed estates, slate quarries and mines all of which were in decline, Jack was a new broom. His was a far sighted vision of the future. Without him we would not still have the world famous narrow gauge railways which were in serious decline when Jack arrived. The Snowdon Highland Railway which has only recently been re-opened would have been lost years ago without him. Many of his plans never came to fruition – some were impractical, but he personally did well out of these enterprises with substantial shareholdings in various companies.

His was a broad brush, sweeping aside details. He did not inspire trust – he was viewed as a jumped up newcomer, too big for his boots and resented by many. But he can be said to have been the saviour of ACL. The Haugvik development was to be his last contribution to the fortunes of ACL, in May 1927 he asked to be relieved of his position as Managing Director, claiming that he was near to a nervious breakdown.

He left Plas Maenan in December and was never heard of again in the area. He changed his name to McInnes and died in Tunbridge Wells in 1936.

Products and the Slump

After WW1 the demand for aluminium had grown. It was being increasingly used in the construction of trams and buses, along with commercial vehicles. Aircraft construction was now moving from wood and canvas to machines that used only aluminium. New markets were also developing in the field of domestic products such as saucepans and other items for the kitchen and catering. The rolling mills at Dolgarrog were working day and night, seven days a week to keep up with demand.

However, it was not to last – the dam disaster had punched a big hole in the finances of the Corporation and along came great 1930's slump. A major retrenchment was called for and the Corporation was forced to drastically re-organise. It started with the shares being substantially written down in value, followed by major redundancies in the factory – especially among the heads of departments. In 1931 the business really hit the buffers – the directors agreed to take a 50% cut in their fees and the auditors took a 10% cut. The workers agreed to take a 10% cut in their wages. The Corporation's extensive portfolio of properties and land was put on the market, including Jack's mansion which did not find a buyer. The Porth Llwyd Hotel was leased to the Royal British Legion. Vessels, locomotives, cars and equipment were sold off or scrapped. ACL's holdings in the North Wales Power Company (as it was now known) were sold along with the water rights, dams, pipes, tramways and Cwm Dyli and Maentwrog Power Stations. Even the Dolgarrog Power Station was now to be operated by the newly formed Central Electricity Board.

Chapter 13

Plas Maenan mystery

Plas Maenan – a Mystery

In 1930 ACL put the house up for sale. An estate agent's document of the time lists all the features of the house and tells us that there were extensive cellars which included a central heating furnace. The plans showed no evidence of a very large strongroom being present at that time. There was at least one potential buyer from Liverpool but no sale ensued.

It would appear that an employee of ACL acted as a live-in caretaker, as for this period no rent was paid but there were charges for electricity used, but not every month and the amounts varied considerably.

My friend, the late Jess Yates of television fame, father of the late Paula who married Bob Geldof, told me that it was well known locally that the house had been leased by a group of prominent Llandudno businessmen as an hotel

Plas Maenan

and lovenest for assignations with their floosies. The tunnel provided a discreet entrance and exit to the house. He said that the ladies concerned were dropped off in the lay-by which used to be near the old gate lodge and walked up the old drive to the underground entrance. One might suppose that the directors of ACL might have been party to these arrangements. There is no actual evidence for this but it would be surprising if they did not know!

Come 1938 the house was leased to a lady and in 1946 the house was sold to a lady from Colwyn Bay but we have no information about either of them.

Now scroll on – in the 1970's my friend Hefin Hughes, who was visiting Plas Maenan on business, was met by a couple who had just bought the hotel and were re-decorating the interior. They said:

> you are the second visitor we have had to-day.

Presumably they didn't get many visitors! They then told Hefin about the first visitor. It seems the man, who had been in the army during WW2 had been stationed at nearby Dolgarrog and his job was to guard a strongroom in the cellar of Plas Maenan. He was told that there was a girl's school upstairs (this was the Kent House School evacuated from Sale, Manchester in 1940) and he was warned that he must not be seen by anyone from the school. The ex-soldier took the couple down into the cellar and showed them

The strongroom door

Entrance to tunnel 1

where he had spent many a long night. He had no knowledge of the contents of the strongroom and in those days you didn't ask!

The tunnel which provided the secret access was equipped with a guardroom at the entrance. It is now home to a large colony of Lesser Horseshoe Bats!

To add to the mystery, a former pupil of the school wrote a book about her experiences at Plas Maenan during the war. She tells of the girls walking across the valley to go to church or sometimes a film show in the Dolgarrog Assembly Hall. She recounts how when they moved from Sale the school handyman came with them to settle them in, but left shortly afterwards to return to Sale. No other male was employed from then on.

The furnace in the cellar, which was strictly out of bounds to the girls, was quite obviously being regularly stoked up but there was no stoker! There is a substantial coke bunker at the rear with chutes to take the fuel down to the furnace room. The ex-pupil speculated that maybe the headmistress did it, but concluded that it seemed most unlikely!

The strong room is of a rather unusual design. Many big houses used to have at least a large safe for the valuable silver, but this one is on a totally different scale.This sizeable room which is free-standing within the cellar, has blast proof walls and the door is of the dimensions you would expect to find in a walk in bank vault. These would provide some protection for the contents even in the event an attack with explosives.

Why would anyone install such a strongroom? It certainly wasn't Harry Jack as in 1930 there is no mention of it. From 1930 till 1938 ACL were in no position to finance such a construction and there is no documentary evidence that they did. It would have been a major undertaking. There are clear indications that the floor of the ballroom above it had to be removed to allow the work to be carried out, and then re-instated afterwards. Even the well known supplier of the vault door, Chubb, is not able to provide any information about it.

So who dun it? The minute book of the directors meetings is missing for that year – so no help there. There is still however, the mystery of the whereabouts of the Crown Jewels during the war. It is documented that in about August 1939 one hundred and forty or so items in their custom made leather cases were transported from the Tower of London in a fleet of cars, to Windsor Castle to be deposited in a cellar. This was no doubt just a temporary measure, with war about to be declared and the expected destruction of London by Nazi bombers. Months went by without much happening on the home front and this period became known as the phoney war – lasting until Dunkirk in May 1949 and the start of the Battle of Britain in the July. This gave the government breathing space to arrange for a secure and secret alternative far away from the feared invasion across the Channel by the Nazis.

Plas Maenan would have fitted the bill for such a safe place perfectly. We do know that in 1940 the Government planned to evacuate the King, Queen and Royal family. They were to be transported by car to Liverpool and taken by a fast Navy Destroyer to exile in Canada. The same, no doubt, would have applied to the Crown Jewels so north

Wales would have been the ideal place. After all, in 1941 the treasures of the National Gallery were brought to north Wales for safe storage in a slate mine at Blaenau Ffestiniog. Plas Maenan is within several hundred yards of a railway station so that the precious hoard could have been swiftly transported to Liverpool to meet up with the King and Queen on their way to cross the Atlantic. Security was provided by the army presence at Dolgarrog complete with their anti-aircraft guns.

We know that ACL was considered as strategically important hence, on the face of it, the army contingent was guarding the factory. One of the oddest things is that the army established a Starfish Decoy Site about 2 miles away, 1,000 ft above Dolgarrog on the road to Eigiau. The remains of the control bunker can still be seen. The locals at the time thought that it was there to guard the dams but its real purpose was to light fires to simulate the incendiary bombs dropped by German Pathfinder Bombers. This was quite a

The Star Fish decoy site

common ploy to confuse the attackers who were targetting our major towns and cities.

Strangely, the very large Hotpoint Factory just down the river at Llandudno Junction which was building aircraft wings, had no such protection. It was much more high profile than Dolgarrog yet did not have a military presence or anti-aircraft guns. There were many, possibly more important factories in Britain which did not have their own army guard.

My guess is that this was all a clever charade to hide the fact that the army was really there to protect the national treasures residing in the strong room at Plas Maenan, though they did not know it! The National Archives at Kew say they have no records about such a move. They suggest there were no written records so that Nazi invaders would not have been able to trace the location of the jewels. We can but speculate!

Chapter 14

WW2 and a boom

World War Two

Dolgarrog had a good war – it certainly revived the factory's fortunes. In 1940 the Corporation was informed by the Ministry of Supply that it was to become a controlled undertaking under the Defence Regulations. Security from attack was the first priority. A Drill Hall was built, with the Home Guard manning pill boxes which commanded access to the girder bridge, the factory, the main road and the dams. The houses were painted with camouflage colours and air raid shelters were built in the factory. An observation post was established on the roof of one of the buildings for plane spotting. It was joined by three anti-aircraft guns manned by a regular army unit. One of these was on the road to the Newborough Arms, another by the rail track across the valley, whilst the other was positioned on occasion in the field just below Plas Jack.

The factory was considered to be a vital part of the war effort – being a major producer of aluminium for aircraft construction and additional furnaces were installed. The Ministry of Aircraft Production took a large proportion of the output and in 1942 the Light Metals Control ordered the rolling mill to increase production to 4,750 tons per annum. The Ministry maintained strict controls on the quality of the metal produced.

Both road and rail were used to dispatch the finished product. In 1943 a new steam locomotive arrived and was named *Dolgarrog No 1* and was soon deployed hauling trains of thirty wagons from Dolgarrog Station to the works.

Loco – Dolgarrog No. 1 *with driver Richard Jones and fireman Thomas Roberts*

Many of the male workers were called up for the forces while others, mostly key personnel, were classed as 'reserve occupationists'. ACL, to their credit, remitted the rent on the company houses for those who went into the forces. Women were recruited to take on the work previously the domain of men. Apart from driving fork lift trucks, one woman regularly drove a lorry to Liverpool docks with a consignments of goods. They also worked night shifts.

In 1942 the old Assembly Rooms was burnt to the ground. This was quite serious as it was the only place of entertainment and recreation in the district. To keep up morale the workers needed a place to socialise. This was during a time when all materials and manpower were in short supply, but clearly Sir Stafford Cripps at the Ministry of Aircraft Production saw that this was an emergency situation. He gave permission for a new village hall to be built by ACL near to the Porth Llwyd Bridge, and this was completed in 1943. Films were shown every Tuesday and Friday and it was used as a dance hall on Saturdays. It was the vital social centre of the village which attracted girls from

A visit by Santa Claus to the children of the village, in the Assembly Hall, in December of 1971

up and down the valley, as there was no shortage of adult males! The driver of the Dolgarrog No.1 locomotive was Richard Jones known to the locals as *Dick yr-enjin.* He had an evening job opening and closing the curtains for the cinema shows in the hall and also taught in the Sunday School which was held there. Afterwards he was in the habit of popping over the road to the Legion for a pint until it came to the notice of the church authorities. (In those days Wales was dry on Sundays except for members' clubs!) The church promptly gave him the boot! Sadly now abandoned and derelict, the hall would make an ideal small factory unit to provide local employment. I believe there are still a lot of ex ACL workers who are commuting to Llanberis to work every day.

In 1943 the price of the raw aluminium from Canada at £110 per ton under cut Dolgarrog's cost of more than £300 per ton and at the end of 1943 the War Ministry ordered that ACL should stop the reduction process. One can't help wondering about this! At the height of the Battle of the Atlantic seamen were losing their lives to import aluminium and save the Ministry a few miserable pounds! What a price to pay! Anyway, ACL complied and the furnaces were finally closed down on 1 March 1944. Overall Dolgarrog emerged from the war as a specialist in the rolling and finishing of aluminium, with a reputation of producing a quality product.

In the village the people set about restoring the social and sporting life that they had enjoyed before the war.

There followed a number of management changes, the most significant being that in 1948 Jack Berry joined the Company as Works Manager. He had previously worked for Alcan in Canada and then the British Aluminium Company. With his wealth of experience, in 1965 he became the Managing Director. He was with ACL for 27 years. He died in 1987 having left behind him a business which he had worked strenuously to ensure its continued prosperity. A nicer man you could not have met. During his time at ACL it had been taken over by successive larger rival companies, eventually being owned by Alcan the world's largest aluminium company. This proved to be an advantage as investments were made in the most modern strip mills culminating in the installation, in 1965, of a Loewy 4-Hi constant gap mill which was hailed at the time as being the most advanced aluminium strip rolling equipment in the world. I filmed it for the BBC at the time, for the Wales Today news programme. It was impressive.

Then there was a diversion when ACL recognised that there was a growing market for aluminium for saucepans and frying pans known in the trade as hollowware. In 1969 they installed presses and circle cutters which they then coated with Teflon and other non-stick materials to be sold on to manufacturers of the domestic product. By the late 1970's and early 80's recession hit the business hard. The number of workers was halved compared with the number in 1970, but the investment programme continued to increase the range of specialist alloy products. The opening of the Rio Tinto aluminium smelting plant at Holyhead in 1971, must have been to ACL's advantage. This plant had been built to take a cheap supply of electricity from the new Wylfa nuclear power station on Anglesey.

In 2001, post 9/11, there was a severe downturn in demand for aluminium from the aviation industry and in 2002 the business was put up for sale as a going concern – but there were no takers. It was however, saved by a management buy-out. Sadly that was not to last – in 2007 the rollings mills ground to a halt and the factory finally closed, just a hundred years after the business was founded. The end of an era!

Councillor Dafydd Williams is the long time Chairman of Dolgarrog Community Council. He says, self deprecatingly, that no one else will do the job! He really does deserves the title of 'Mr. Dolgarrog'. A former employee of ACL, he knows the ropes. Using his native Welsh ability of wheeler dealing he has been the prime mover – helped by many other villagers, in establishing a new Post Office and Community Centre in the redundant clinic. The Community Centre contains a Mini-Museum telling the village's story. Alongside is a children's playground, which has been given the title of 'Parc Dafydd' in his honour.

Apart from that, led by Dafydd, the village War Memorial Garden has been vastly improved. But the biggest project has been the new Memorial bearing the names of all those who lost their lives in the dam disaster. And visitors can now follow the newly constructed walkway to gaze in wonder upon the gigantic boulders swept down in the flood.

Chapter 15

End of the line and a new beginning

A Second Coming

Just before the banks crashed in 2008 the Wigan family, most famously known in the north-west as owners of Ainscough Crane Hire, sold that business and moved into strategic land development. The group retained one company which was a specialist factory demolition and recycling business, run by Matt Ainscough. His company tendered for the demolition of the ACL factory. When the site was cleared they bought it as a land deal to develop it for leisure or mixed use, with the prospect that they might be able build lodges or provide a caravan site. Andy Ainscough, who is a surfing enthusiast, saw the potential for a Wavegarden with Spanish designed technology. The family formed the company Surf Snowdonia to build the world's only Wavegarden surfing lake which promised to create new life for Dolgarrog. This proved to be less than easy, a Dolgarrog tradition! Much initial decontamination work had to be undertaken, following a century of use as an industrial site. Over 25,000 cubic metres of on-site material was crushed and re-used during the construction, including the recycling of 400 tonnes of steel, cast iron and copper. 6.3 miles of piling was driven into the ground to stabilise it. Work was completed in 2015 at a cost of £12 million. The pool is nearly 1,000 ft in length and was the longest man made surfing wave in the World. However, this record was short lived because a bigger one was recently constructed in Texas. Damn those Yanks! Still, Surf Snowdonia is the largest one in Europe and can be used by 38 surfers at one time. About 120 people are employed during the season, some of them former ACL workers. In addition they have a Crash and Splash pool and a camp site with 36 wooden camping pods. They are considering building an hotel as well.

Andy is the Managing Director and his father is the Company Chairman so it is truly a family run business. It has proved to be an instant success, in their first two weeks there were 14,000 visitors and last year, 2017, they had a record attendance of over 150,000.

I reckon that even Harry Jack would be impressed, could he see it now!

Acknowledgements

Dolgarrog Industrial History, Eric Jones & David Gywn. Gwynedd Archives 1989 – a veritable mine of information.

Sue Ellis and her helpful staff at Conwy County Archives, Llandudno

My friend Hefin Hughes who helped me with the field work

Dafydd Williams, Chairman, Dolgarrog Community Council, and numerous residents of the the village who have shared passed down family stories

Adrian Hughes, Llandudno Home Front Museum, for his help concerning mititary matters

Andy Ainscough, Managing Director of Surf Snowdonia, for his help bringing things up-to-date

And last but by no means least Barbara, my wife – an author in her own right, for her help in the seemingly endless task of getting the text ready for publication!